PRAISE FOR **Hope Upon Impact**

"An uplifting testament to the power of prayer and perseverance. Overlease and her family share their journey of healing, always directing the reader back to the hope they found in the consoling prayers and support of so many people all across the country. This book speaks to the power of love through prayer and service. Prayer changes things. It heals and restores, renews, and rebuilds. Evelyn is proof of its sustaining grace."

—MARY E. LENABURG, author of *Be Brave in the Scared: How I Learned to Trust God during the Most Difficult Days of My Life*

"This is one of the most amazing books I've had the honor of reading! Julie Overlease's heartfelt story of her daughter's horrible accident and recovery, as well as the strong faith of her family and friends, left me speechless, thankful, and full of hope. She has the ability to capture the moment and draw on the emotions that cause you to feel as though you are in that exact moment with her. You will laugh, cry, pray, hope, and cheer!"

—LES NORMAN, retired MLB player for the Kansas City Royals, and host of the syndicated "Breakin' the Norm" radio show

"For many, finding a cause for hope amidst tragedy feels impossible. When her young daughter Evelyn suffered a traumatic brain injury, Julie Overlease managed to find faith amidst her fear and to see evidence of God's omnipresent love at every turn. By sharing her family's journey, Overlease offers encouragement and inspiration for anyone facing obstacles, providing an important reminder that even in the hardest moments of life, we never journey alone."

—LISA M. HENDEY, author of *I Am God's Storyteller*

"*Hope Upon Impact* reaffirms that we are to trust God at all costs. Julie Overlease reminds us in a heartfelt and moving way, through her experience of spending time with God, understanding that God's will is not necessarily ours, and surrendering ourselves, all can become whole through the power of Jesus. I am reminded that mercy is not so much something God has, as God *is*."

—FR. JIM SICHKO, Evangelist and Papal Missionary of Mercy for Pope Francis

❧

"Twelve-year-old Evelyn's freak injury resulting in a traumatic brain injury became the occasion for a deepened faith for her parents, family and friends. This is the story of faithful parental love, of a community of faith surrounding a hurting family with compassion, care and prayers, and ultimately a testimony of hope in God's providence. This memoir chronicles how, for the person of faith, God provides many consolations and signs of his love in the midst of the unexpected and terrifying storms of life."

—ARCHBISHOP JOSEPH F. NAUMANN, Archbishop of Kansas City in Kansas

❧

"*Hope Upon Impact* testifies, like soldiers restarting their lives after war, that it's not the tragedy that strictly determines the outcome of events, but how we react. Overlease's inspiring account of love, community, and faith in a beneficent God is not only a joy to read, but vividly portrays the interplay of the saving power of all three, separate roots to the Tree of Life. The truth is, it's not important in the final analysis what the tragedy was. Whether you are a person of deep faith or an atheist, you can't help but admire, be humanly moved and inspired by the outcomes. If strength overcoming terrifying adversity can illuminate life's most meaningful path forward, Overlease's faithful journey will shine a beacon through the jungle, right after you wipe the tears of pain, gratitude, and joy from your eyes."

—RABBI MARK H. LEVIN, D.H.L., Founding Rabbi of Congregation Beth Torah (Overland Park, KS); author of *Praying the Bible*

Hope Upon Impact

A Miraculous True Story of Faith, Love, & God's Goodness

JULIE OVERLEASE

PARACLETE PRESS
BREWSTER, MASSACHUSETTS

For Robbie, our children,
those I hold dear,
and all who "Hope on!"

2020 First Printing

Hope Upon Impact: A Miraculous True Story of Faith, Love, & God's Goodness

Copyright © 2020 by Julie Overlease

ISBN 978-1-64060-410-0

The Paraclete Press name and logo (dove on cross) are trademarks of Paraclete Press, Inc.

Library of Congress Cataloging-in-Publication Data
Names: Overlease, Julie, 1974- author.
Title: Hope upon impact : a miraculous true story of faith, love, and God's
  goodness / Julie Overlease.
Description: Brewster, Massachusetts : Paraclete Press, 2020. | Includes
  bibliographical references. | Summary: "A mother's story of faith in
  action and the goodness of God, as her child recovers from a devastating
  blow to the head"-- Provided by publisher.
Identifiers: LCCN 2019043682 | ISBN 9781640604100 (hardcover) | ISBN
  9781640604117 (mobi) | ISBN 9781640604124 (epub) | ISBN 9781640604131
  (pdf)
Subjects: LCSH: Overlease, Julie, 1974- | Brain--Wounds and
  injuries--Patients--United States--Biography. |
  Skull--Fractures--Patients--United States--Biography. | Accident
  victims--Family relationships--United States--Biography. | Mothers and
  dauthers. | Prayer--Christianity.
Classification: LCC RD594 .O84 2020 | DDC 617.4/81044092 [B]--dc23
LC record available at https://lccn.loc.gov/2019043682

10 9 8 7 6 5 4 3 2 1

Published by Paraclete Press
Brewster, Massachusetts
www.paracletepress.com

Printed in the United States of America

Contents

Appendix:

This is a true story of faith, love, and God's goodness. The greatest of these is love because God is love. With God, all things are possible. That belief manifested itself as truth through the journey of my daughter Evelyn's experience. Many people have called it a miracle.

Evelyn's amazing story is one of true friendship and love—friendship among adolescent girls, among fellow parents, and among neighbors, and connections made among people all over the United States. This is a story of God's profound love, the sincere devotion and loving support of family, and friends who treat us like family. This is a story of a young girl's crazy love for her puppy; her instinctive bravery to protect him; the tragedy of a severe, freak, and most perilous accident; and the experience of living through the difficult aftermath. This is the story of the tremendous power of prayer—a true prayer army storming the heavens to fight for the life of my daughter.

Through this experience, we received an overwhelming show of support from a vast community of the faithful. Through the gift of our faith and confidence in God's love and goodness, we maintained a deep sense of inner peace and abundant hope in the face of adversity and uncertain outcomes. Happily, this is the story of a precious little sister's First Communion, which turned out to be incredibly extra special in the wake of a tragic family crisis. Above all, it is a story of hoping in the Lord, trusting his holy will after a devastating blow, and feeling secure in every form of love known to the soul.

This is an account of the impact of Evelyn's accident. It has taken all of us—family, friends, and strangers alike—from weeping and despair to delightful, unexpected laughter and joy. We were thrust onto a wild, unexpected ride on a recent April day, and within my heart, in spite of the struggle, we have emerged stronger in a multitude of ways that matter deep within the core of our beings.

Good has come of Evelyn's accident and her suffering. Of this I am certain.

Life can change forever in a single second, and we may find ourselves at a turning point where we will always have a "before" and "after." This can be extremely hard. However, I believe there is meaning in every trial. Seek it. Look for God's light in times of darkness. He is everywhere. Aim to change the world one personal connection at a time by being the light of Christ through loving acts to those who need it. With faith and trust in God, I encourage everyone to "Hope on!" That inspiring command has been in my heart since I first heard the phrase years ago in a Scripture study discussion with women I deeply respect and have come to cherish. Little did I know that "Hope on!" would become more than my mental mantra when faced with a crisis. "Hope on!" would ring as a spiritual battle cry when it seemed that all was lost. That hope was in my fiber, and it sustained me.

"Have no anxiety at all, but in everything, by prayer and petition, with thanksgiving, make your requests known to God. Then the peace of God that surpasses all understanding will guard your hearts and minds in Christ Jesus." —Philippians 4:6–7

Chapter 1

Begin at the Beginning

Unforeseen in a sliver of a moment…a juncture, the path parts,
Flung in one direction against our will,
An incalculable journey begins,
Wrought with vast unknowns,
Left to grapple with all that is yet unrevealed.
Distant, transcendent abundance, now blurred by trees, awaits.
Release the clench, acquiesce, resolve to emerge victorious.
Believe in ensuing good with certitude.
Hope on!

. . . . *June 12, 2018*

While I was alone on a run early in the morning, the song "Time of Your Life" by Green Day randomly played on my old-school iPod "Run!" playlist. I had not heard it in many years, and the lyrics hit me like a ton of bricks. I began sobbing on the sidewalk, stopped dead in my tracks, and I was thankful that the song didn't begin until I happened to be walking in cool-down mode.

My little brother, Anthony Niedzielski, was diagnosed with Acute Myelogenous Leukemia on January 28, 2000. Only nineteen years old, he was in his freshman year at Purdue University. During his cancer battle, Anthony learned how to play the guitar, which had been a dream and goal of his for many years. Music became a form of therapeutic medicine during Anthony's fight for his life, and it brought him comfort at a time when nearly nothing else could. He made me a CD of his favorite guitar songs, which I treasure. "Good Riddance (Time of Your Life)" is on it. The lyrics were so moving at the time of Anthony's illness. My dear brother has the uncanny ability to make me belly laugh nearly every time we communicate. My only blood sibling, I could not imagine losing him while he was still a teenager. I pleaded with God to save Anthony. Almost two decades later, he's alive and well—a thriving, professional, happily married man, and an incredibly fun uncle. Now the meaning of the song's words applies to Evelyn's accident, as well. Life is funny like that. Music, emotionally transcending and deeply moving, has the power to touch us at our core.

My family definitely hit a turning point when faced with a totally unpredictable calamity. No one saw it coming. No warning. It was the ultimate test—first and foremost, physically and medically for Evelyn, yet also emotionally for those who were present when it happened, and spiritually for all of us. We learned countless lessons about ourselves, our community, and the true source of our strength and comfort: our God.

However, I must back up. I remember when my young children— Olivia, Evelyn, Henry, and Vivian—expressed their heart's desire for a puppy. That is the beginning of this uncommon and marvelous story. I had never had a dog and felt little affinity for dogs. Truthfully, I thought most dogs were rather stinky. I wished to avoid the responsibility of caring for one since I had recently reached the parenting milestone in which my youngest child attended full-day school. However, the absolutely unadulterated joy that shone on the faces of my children changed me after spending a weekend with two little dogs, Vito and Lola, on a stay with extended family. The kids' happiness was infectious. For the first time in my life, I was open to the notion of a four-legged family pet.

The kids begged, and offered outlandish deals to their dad, Robbie, including, "Dad, if I can learn to play the whole *William Tell* Overture on the piano, will you get us a dog?" And, "Dad, if I break the cross-country city record for my age group, will you let us get a dog?" "Sure," he'd slyly say with a smile. This went on for over a year. We liked their gumption and admired their persistence.

On Christmas morning, our children discovered a special gift inside an otherwise-empty dog crate under our tree. They excitedly tore into the package and discovered photos of an adorable male puppy with a note that he would join our family at eight weeks of age in early February, near our youngest's seventh birthday. Our children excitedly counted down the days until their puppy joined our family. Robbie suggested the name Winston. I liked Clive, the name of a Houston restaurant with a funny story behind it. Evelyn wanted to name him Bear since he looked like a teddy bear. We voted.

On Saturday, February 4, 2017, Evelyn, our second eldest, strolled into our bedroom, blissfully anticipating meeting the puppy. She cheerfully belted out, with extra loud and pitch-perfect singing, that it was going to be the best day of her life. Evelyn made us chuckle, and her utter joy was boldly displayed on her exuberant face. Our family drove three hours and parked to wait for the breeder from Krista's Poodles to arrive with our puppy.

Krista pulled up next to our minivan in a farm pickup truck with our miniature red poodle nuzzled against her chest. The kids leapt from our vehicle, and Krista gingerly emerged from her truck. She looked me in the eyes and presented me, the mama of our clan, with our first four-legged family member.

I gazed into Winston Bear's sweet, brown, puppy dog eyes, and I fell in love at first sight. Quick to cry when happy, I found my eyes filled with tears as she placed him in my arms. He was truly darling. I melted. His coat was soft and fluffy, the beautiful autumn color of fallen oak leaves. I loved the way he smelled, fresh like shampoo. He was warm and little, still and quiet. I, who never wanted a dog, was instantly and totally enamored. Best of all, my sweet husband announced I got the first turn holding Winston on the drive home.

As much as each child desired a pet, I think Evelyn wanted one most of all. She and Winston walked, played, and snuggled. Through their time spent together they developed a delightfully special bond and sweet affection. As the one with the most time at home with him, feeding and regularly meeting his basic needs, I consider myself his favorite, but Evelyn would vehemently dispute this. My daughter adores her puppy, and she demonstrated that deep love through her actions when tragedy struck on a fateful spring day. We never know what life has in store for us until we must live it. We never know what choices we will make until we are faced with them.

"There is no greater love than to lay down one's life for one's friends."
—John 15:13 (NLT)

Chapter 2

Evelyn's Accident

Sometimes in life, people are faced with moments that change everything. It can be difficult to stay upright when life does not go as planned, careening drastically off course. The heaviness of our suffering and the deepness of our despair threaten to crumple us like paper, further flattened by the sheer weight and unstoppable momentum of a life event. In an instant, everything can turn into an upside-down mess, and we may ask ourselves, "How can I handle this?" or "Will order ever be restored?" So in our anguish we must remember to turn our gaze to God and hold fast to him. Faith has the power to sustain us through the great storms of life.

Many lives have been touched through the account you are reading. Something powerful was waiting in the wings with the potential to bless our sweet, carefree, young daughter. We floundered helplessly and struggled, yet we discovered that countless blessings, including beauty and grace, may result from enduring terrible challenges one would never choose to face.

The same is true for you. We all may find strength to face fear and courage to simply take the next good step with the security that we never walk alone. God will lovingly show us the magnitude of our ability to face difficulties in partnership with him if only we surrender and trust. We must lay the tough matters at his feet, for in spite of our best efforts or attitudes to the contrary, we are powerless. Self-reliance is not enough. I know this from experience.

Friday, April 20, 2018, was a day off school for my three younger children. First Communion was scheduled the next morning for our youngest child, Vivian, a second grader. I had spent the entire week preparing to host friends and loved ones for a big celebration after

Saturday's Mass. My father, Tom Niedzielski, and stepmom, Jane, arrived the previous afternoon from Springfield, Illinois, in time to watch our oldest child, 14-year-old Olivia, race the open 400 meters at the Rockhurst High School Invitational in Kansas City, Missouri, for Notre Dame de Sion High School. It was Olivia's first track meet back after a break from competing due to an injury. Her coaches and family members were excited to see what she could do after rest and rehabilitation efforts. Olivia ran a good race that Thursday afternoon, and it was a perfect day.

Each of my younger children, Vivian (8), Henry (almost 10), and Evelyn (newly 12), had late-morning plans with friends. Henry and Vivian would attend separate activities with classmates. Evelyn had been invited to see a movie, *The Miracle Season*, about a high-school volleyball player who died suddenly and the effect her passing had on her team. The eight sixth-grade girls planning to see the movie would go back to Macy Goodman's home for pizza, and then they were invited to hang out until 4:30 PM. I told Evelyn that she could see the movie and eat lunch with her friends, but she had to compromise by returning home to spend time with her grandparents, since they were in town. That sounded fine to her.

When my dad reflected on that day, he shared, "Friday morning Julie noted that Evelyn was intending to visit some friends at the home of one of them, some blocks away. Jane and I said we would be glad to walk with her to the friend's home, and walk back, getting in a bit of exercise in the process. Julie thought that this would be a fine idea, so when the time came to proceed, the three of us made the walk, enjoying the moments with Evelyn along the way. As Jane and I walked back, we shared our recognition of the growth physically and emotionally of the children and the development of each one's unique personality."

That afternoon, Allie Goodman, Macy's mom, kept me in the loop about their return to the house after the movie; she texted me once the girls finished lunch. I told her I would head that way to pick up Evelyn. I mentioned this to Dad and Jane, and he suggested that rather than drive, he walk with me to get Evelyn. It was a pretty day in the low 60s Fahrenheit. I wore an insulated vest, and Grandma Jane, who decided to join us, threw on a black fleece vest. I decided to take our puppy, Winston. He always got excited when he heard the word "walk."

As Henry and Vivian groaned about not wanting to walk with us, the kitchen door from the garage opened. Robbie arrived home from his twice-monthly half-day of work. On other Fridays of the month Robbie works in Sedalia, Missouri, an hour and a half from home. On this day, his timing was perfect. I could leave the two little kids home with their dad. I kissed Robbie goodbye, and we were off! We then proceeded at a leisurely pace for Dad's sake.

My father was t-boned on his motorcycle a half block from our home at an intersection in front of our church when I was just a year old. He broke an arm and multiple ribs, shattered his right leg, smashed his face and wrist, and spent a month in a coma and 104 days in the hospital. He spent another six months at home in a hospital bed and had to learn how to walk again. Dad still walks with a slight limp, which is why we took our time moving up Delmar Street to the Goodmans' home that Friday. We visited on our way and enjoyed the spring day without so much as the slightest hint of the disaster that would shatter the peace of our happy world in a matter of minutes. Life would never be the same again. We never know what fate awaits us around the bend.

We arrived at the Goodmans' home, and two moms, Kelli Martin and Allie, were standing in the driveway chatting. Evelyn ran up with a big grin and a quick, "Hey, Mom!" I remember the twinkle of mischief in her blue eyes as she took the red leash and happily scooped up her puppy before running into the fenced backyard to play with the other girls. I made introductions and we visited for a few minutes.

Two girls were playing tennis over a portable tennis-court net. I commented on how the Goodmans had such an awesome flat and expansive driveway with a great basketball goal and space for the kids to play. I then said, "Well, I need to grab Ev. Robbie is home with the little kids, and we need to walk home to relieve him so he can pick up Olivia from Sion for her physical-therapy appointment." I took two steps toward the backyard. Just then, a tremendous "crack!" sound exploded in the air like a shotgun. Time and conversation stopped as all eyes turned to the source of the unexpected, ear-splitting, terrifying noise.

In the backyard stood a tall tree with a major section of limb on the trunk starting to fall, pivoting from its connection point high on the main trunk in a 7 o'clock direction toward us. "NO! No, no, no," raged the voice in my head. A wooden privacy fence blocked the view of what was happening with the girls in the backyard, as we adults were in the safety of the open driveway. I took off running toward the fence, and through the horizontal slats of the modern-style wooden structure I could see the frantic movement of girls in brightly colored clothes running toward the fence.

I screamed to the girls, "Is everyone safe? Is everyone safe?!" A sickening feeling arose in my being as a thunderous sound reverberated through the air the moment the great tree limb crashed down, thudding against the earth with the force and power reserved for things of nature. As I reached the fence, I could see through the slats that Evelyn was on the ground in a still heap. I felt utter despair.

I recognized her clothes. Fear unfurled within me, and my heart took off at a gallop, every single nerve in my body on high alert, but I was impeded by the fence from making the slightest bit of forward progress. All thumbs, I clumsily and desperately tried to open the gate to access the backyard, but in my panic I couldn't figure out how to undo the latch on their fence gate! My brain wouldn't work. I fumbled. That physical barrier was horrible. Time shifted to an agonizing slow motion, and my heart pounded as though it would burst inside my chest. I wanted to bash through the wood with my bare hands. I wanted to leap over it to rescue my girl. I wanted to do anything to get past that damn barrier. "For the love of God, I just need to go to my daughter!" screamed the voice in my head in pure terror. A second later, for I am sure that is all the time it took, someone else opened the gate and I raced to Evelyn with adrenaline surging.

I felt like I took a wrecking ball to the heart when the full sight of the scene was before me. My little girl. This couldn't be happening. She was on the ground, motionless and silent, in a duck-and-cover sort of tornado-drill position. Her lower legs from her knees to the tops of her feet were on the ground, tucked beneath the rest of her small body, which was collapsed in a ball. However, her hands and arms were not in the position to protectively shield her head as we had been taught in elementary-school disaster-preparedness drills. They were wrapped around her puppy, whose head was peeking out, gasping for air, panting and shaking, sandwiched and suffocating between Evelyn's thighs and chest. Her torso was folded forward limply over Winston, crushing him into her thighs. Facedown in this fetal position, her forehead was practically touching the ground, and we couldn't see her face. We saw blood on the top of her head.

The scene was too hard to interpret. Evelyn was in the midst of a tremendous mess of broken tree limbs with long bare branches covering her in a myriad of directions. There were leaves and wood shards. My first thoughts were, "Oh, dear God! Did she survive? Is the tree on top of her? Is she being crushed and we must move the tree limb? How are we going to lift a fallen tree?!"

There was a lot of splintered wood covering the ground. A ten-foot-long section of a major limb had crash-landed on the grass by Evelyn. The end of the hefty limb that likely struck Evelyn's head was jagged as though a monster had ripped it in two, violently shredding the severed ends. On the other side of the fractured tree, another long stretch of tapering tree limb confused the scene with broken chunks of wood beside it. I saw a ton of long, bare, sticklike and wispy branches extending from the fallen limbs where she lay. It looked helter-skelter. The stick limbs jutted out in every direction—tons of them. I couldn't tell what was going on, for the scene was a jumbled, puzzling mess of tree debris, and my lack of mental clarity and inability to comprehend the scene made my mind race. I know I processed it all in a second or two, yet I felt helpless that my reaction did not feel instantaneously proactive. I was her mother. It was my duty to rescue her from this accident. I had to act and act fast.

I quickly and gladly ascertained that Evelyn was parallel to a major limb, not beneath one. Evelyn's grandpa pulled the long, branching section of limb away from where she lay to clear the area. Evelyn's chin was tucked to her chest, and her long, light hair was bloody and flipped over her head, falling forward and spilling onto the ground.

Allie said urgently that we needed to get the dog out of her arms. The thought flashed through my head that I didn't care about the dog, I cared about Evelyn, "my child." I think Allie saw him as impeding us and obstructing our view of Evelyn's face, and her intention was to get him out of the way. My puppy looked at me with intense distress in his eyes. His whole body shook violently, and somehow Allie lifted Evelyn's shoulder enough to pull Winston from where he was being smashed in Evelyn's arms against her body.

I heard someone yell, "Call 911!! Call 911!" Robbie's name was mentioned, and I reached for my phone, but it was no longer in my back pocket. My dad and Jane were standing over us, and Dad said his mobile, a flip phone, wouldn't work. 911 told him to try again later, and this incensed me. This simply COULD NOT BE. Not now! Not here in this yard with this accident. NO. I felt a dark and tremendous wave of panic rising when I heard that.

I yelled, "Where is my phone?!" Allie plucked it from the grass where it had fallen, smacked it into my hand, and I surprisingly deftly pressed buttons to call Robbie. By the ultimate grace of God, my husband answered immediately. God wink. He virtually never feels his phone vibrate or answers when I call. "A tree fell and hit Evelyn! COME!! YOU HAVE TO COME! COME!!!" I screamed into the phone.

Evelyn's hair was down and loose at the time of the accident, and it hung bloody and covered her whole face as we tried to assess her seemingly lifeless heap of a body. She started barely moaning, a sign of life! Thank God. Then, she moved erratically, writhed in pain, and unfolded herself from the fetal position with her own power and anguished movements. The terrible sounds of agony that emerged from my little girl roared loud and primal. Her cries told all present the mind-blowing intensity of her heightened pain and suffering. My thoughts begged her to stop making those awful noises, knowing terrible pain was the source, but she continued.

I sank into a seated position on the ground with my legs straight out in a V. Evelyn writhed around on the ground and ended up in a position similar to my own between my legs, her back to my chest. I enveloped her. With my right hand I rested the left side of her face against my right breast. With that same hand, I compressed the top right side of her skull with the fleece vest my stepmom ripped off to slow the bleeding from her lacerated scalp.

With my left hand I tried to move Evelyn's hair out of her face so that I could see her. Once I brushed the mess of hair, damp with blood, to the side of her face, I was struck by the most horrible sight imaginable to a parent. Again, my mind raged a screaming, "No!"

My child's eyes were glassy and wild, yet totally unseeing. Blank. Wrong. They pointed in mad directions, and there was no recognition or awareness in them. They registered intense pain, distress, and shock. They looked like the eyes of someone about to die, as though her precious life were slipping away before my very eyes. She wailed forcefully and gutturally. She bellowed, racked with pain. She seemed blind and deaf, completely unable to hear or respond to anything we said, even when my face was before her or my lips were near her ear. It was horrifying. I was gripped with terror. Death was standing over us. Boldly waiting.

My mind shot to a party last July where another school mother spoke about a terrible fall her son had taken from a tree at Boy Scout camp. He hit his head on a rock, and Mary Kuklenski said that the Whitmore boy, Jake, saved her son's life because he didn't let Eddie go to sleep at the accident. The serious nature of his injuries caused him to be transported by life flight out of the remote campground. This came to mind, and I didn't stop talking. "Evelyn, I love you. Evelyn, stay awake. You have to fight. Hail Mary, full of grace, the Lord is with thee!! Evelyn, I LOVE YOU! EVELYN. EVELYN!"

My next gut-wrenching thought was that if my child were going to die in that yard, then she was going to die in the loving arms of her mother. She would feel my touch, and I would give her all the security possible under horrendous circumstances. It was awful beyond what words may ever adequately convey. My heart was breaking, and I felt filled with despair at the seriousness of the dreadful situation. I held her with all my might and willed her to live but felt powerless. I could not fix this. All I had to offer was a mother's love, human touch, and prayer.

Robbie arrived within minutes and stood over us dumbfounded, trying to make sense of the unthinkable, slowly turning his head and body to take in the massive fallen limb, the mess of tree debris, looking at his bleeding child whose eyes were all wrong, and me—his wife, frantic, hands and clothes covered in his daughter's blood. He clutched his head with both hands. He stared in dismay. The scene was terrible, awful, simply incomprehensible. Hysterical with fright, I screamed in anguish to my husband, "I don't know what to do! I DON'T KNOW WHAT TO DO!!!"

He dropped to the ground before our daughter and started talking to her in a very direct tone. "Evelyn, look at me!" he said with his face right before hers. Again, she would not respond in any manner that allowed us to believe she could see or hear us. Robbie is an ophthalmologist, and her eyes were unnerving to him; they did not present in a way that fit any differential that rolled through his brain as he rapidly clipped through life-threatening diagnostic possibilities. Evelyn's eyes looked terribly wrong. Then, she started screaming.

She had been moaning in pain, and that sound was awful enough. When she started screaming things got worse. Evelyn's right hand and arm reached up toward her head in a frantic clawing motion as though trying uncontrollably and erratically to swipe her bloody hair out of her face. I looked down and saw a ghastly, bloody, open wound on the top of her right foot. Evelyn then began kicking madly, thrashing violently with her right leg, thrusting her right heel forward, then bending and pulling her knee toward her chest repeatedly. I kept telling her I loved her.

The paramedics arrived in the backyard. They quickly grabbed under Evelyn's armpits and legs and hoisted her roughly, like a sack of potatoes, onto the stretcher without following any protocol to protect against spinal-cord injury. That seemed odd and wrong, even with my limited knowledge about proper procedures in such instances and in my impaired mental state after facing an emergency. I wondered if my child was in good hands.

Out of my peripheral vision to the left several feet away, I glimpsed my puppy on his side, quivering and convulsing. Allie said urgently, "Julie, we need to get your puppy to a vet." "Dad, there's a vet by Peach Wave across from school," I shot back in a flash. Dad stood motionless, arms hanging down at his sides, face expressionless, seemingly in shock. Allie told him there was an animal clinic nearby. I thought with disbelief and deep dread as I hurriedly prepared to leave the yard, "What is happening?! Please let my little girl live! God help us. Our puppy is going to die? I can't believe what has happened. My puppy can't die on top of everything else. This is all too much."

I stood and quickly followed the stretcher out of the yard, noticing that Evelyn's left eye was now black and swollen. That was a cause for alarm since it could indicate bleeding within her skull and brain damage. I saw Ashley Daly-Murphy, MD, the mother of Evelyn's friend, Lauryn, on her phone as I exited the yard. As a pediatric hospitalist for Children's Mercy Hospital in Kansas City, she had access to an inside employee line. I later learned that she identified herself, then said, "I am calling in a trauma from a backyard. Assemble a trauma team. . . ."

I was on the wildest ride of my life, but I didn't understand that this was not merely metaphorical, but was instead about to turn decidedly literal.

Our unforgettable ambulance ride to the hospital was outrageous in its sheer lunacy. I was ignorant to the shocking rage that was before me— the maddening anxiety that would surge and course through my body and seize me in something much deeper and darker than fear. I was at the mercy of three men, yet no other option existed. How would this end? A precious young life rested in the balance. I was a desperate woman with no control on the brink of hell.

"Ah, could my anguish but be measured and my calamity laid with it in the scales, They would now outweigh the sands of the sea!"—Job 6:2–3

Chapter 3

"Drive Faster!"

What happened next was like an awful joke—the ugliest, worst, most ironic sort of joke one could play on a mother in crisis. The ambulance driver told me to get into the passenger seat, which I did. Robbie had to drive on his own, as only one parent was allowed in the front seat of the ambulance. He could not follow us per protocol, or the ambulance driver couldn't "go hot." There was an open area between the back of the ambulance and the cab. The driver was punching things into his phone and into a GPS-type mounted map screen.

"We are going to Children's Mercy Downtown," I said. He consulted his map. "Do you know how to get to the hospital?!" I urgently implored. He told me he did, but he was asking a guy in back questions that immediately convinced me it was his maiden voyage as an ambulance driver. I was filled with utter dread during the most desperate and vitally important ride of a lifetime.

Illogically, I thought about offering to drive. I asked myself how it was possible that at the most critical moment of my daughter's life we should be in the hands of an ambulance driver who didn't know how to get to the main children's hospital!

I sent out an urgent plea via text at 2:59 PM with shaking hands, Friday, April 20, to eight people (Emily Finlason, Anthony, Mom, Mike Conlon, Jenny McGinnis, Nada Coleman, Sarah Parrish, Adrienne Doring) that said, "Ev in ambulance. Huge tree fell and struck her head. Conscious but unresponsive, head bleeding, major eye swelling—pray!!!!!" They did.

I called my dear friend Jane Hill from the parked ambulance and gave her a quick report. She was working as a speech pathologist to children with special needs thirty minutes away in Lee's Summit that day. She immediately and calmly told me she would meet us at the ER. My brother called me. I don't even remember our exchange, I was so upset.

The driver turned south on Roe Boulevard. I was incensed. Loudly and firmly, I screamed at him: "WE ARE GOING TO CHILDREN'S DOWNTOWN! WHY ARE YOU GOING SOUTH, WHEN THE HOSPITAL IS NORTH?" The hospital was northeast of our location about fourteen miles away. He told me he wanted to take the highway loop, 435. We approached 95th Street on Roe Boulevard, and I told him that Roe was closed southbound for construction without highway access. "You are causing me so much anxiety by going SOUTH when we need to go NORTH. YOU CAN'T GET THROUGH THIS WAY!" He then turned WEST (when we needed to go east), and headed to Nall Avenue to proceed farther south to reach an on ramp to 435. Cars were not getting over.

"I love you, Evelyn. Hang on! Be strong. We're getting help. I love you, Evelyn! Jesus loves you, Evelyn!" I called this out to her again and again over the course of the ride, and the man tending to her said she could hear me. It felt like the ambulance driver was not traveling hot—at all. It was terrible. I wanted to slam my foot onto his accelerator and propel us onward at rocket speed.

Once we got on 435 we made our way into the left lane, but we were still not speeding. When we hit Highway 71 I thought I was going to totally lose my mind. The driver kept consulting his cell phone map. There was a lot of traffic, and everything was congested, each lane nearly packed and slow going. I raised my voice as I beseeched them, "You need do to SOMETHING to get these people the HELL OUT OF OUR WAY!!!!!!" The guy in the back moved slowly forward and nonchalantly, "Oh, we have this rumbler." He shifted a lever forward, and in addition to the whirring siren, an extra layer of loud rumbling siren sounded. I gave stink eye to each car we passed that had impeded our progress. Reader, if there is an ambulance coming up behind you—get yourself out of the way, and do it fast! Lives are at stake!

Then the driver and guy in back started to discuss which exit to take. I contemplated reaching over the driver, opening the door onto the highway, placing my foot firmly on his torso, and giving him a solid kick out the driver-side door, to take over the wheel of the ambulance. My rational thinking calmed my voice, and I seriously said, "Would it be helpful for me to pull up the hospital's location on my phone and direct you there?" I was impressed with my poise given the dire circumstances. A sailor's red streak could have emerged just as easily. He claimed he was okay, assured me he knew where to go. Whatever! I was about to come unglued. How in the world could the driver NOT KNOW HOW TO GET MY CHILD TO THE MAIN CHILDREN'S HOSPITAL IN THE METRO?! Did he know how critical her condition was? I thought, "If my child dies in the back of this ambulance before we get her to a hospital for help, I am going to live a bitter life. I can't handle this!! Hurry up! Go! Move it! Get us there!" I felt so terribly afraid.

Once they decided on an exit, after back-and-forth discussion, 33rd Street versus 22nd Street, they started debating which surface streets to use. My heart rate again increased. My respirations became shallow and rapid. My hands went numb, and my fingers tingled with a panic attack rising. I have had one panic attack in my life, and it occurred after receiving awful news about my brother's medical condition during his leukemia battle. At the time, I thought I was having a heart attack or stroke, and Robbie rushed me to the hospital in the Houston medical center. This time, I understood my body's reaction to stress, but I couldn't moderate the physical effects.

"Take Charlotte?" the driver asked the man in back. I thought, "This CAN'T be happening!" The man in back told the driver he would need to overshoot the hospital, then U-turn back to enter the ER. He didn't swing the ambulance wide enough. Honest. The ambulance came to a stop with the wheels at an angle to the curb. He didn't hop the curb. He braked. He stopped. In slow motion, he shifted into reverse. He slowly crossed his arms, Driver's Ed style, left over right, left over right. Enough! I seethed with bewildered frustration and anger that he would not drive like Evelyn's life depended on it, because it truly did.

A mother in emotional distress has her limits, and mine had been reached. I raised my voice, and in a powerful, intense, commanding, drill-sergeant tone I quickly yelled out, "Do you men have children?!" "Yeah, (pause) I do," and "I have two," they nonchalantly responded. Then I bellowed with a screaming fury that overflowed from the depths of my mama-bear soul with a demanding vengeance that better be heeded, "THEN DRIVE FAASTERRRRRR!" I raged.

They then had the audacity to calmly tell me that if they drove faster and wrecked, we would all be in worse shape. In hindsight, I'm impressed with myself for not uttering any profanity, not one foul word, when faced with such a maddening ride for desperately needed medical help. At long last, Evelyn's ambulance pulled into the ER back entrance of world-renowned Children's Mercy Hospital. The men may have just been trying to do their jobs, and I was not privy to the medical treatment they were providing in the back, but in my hysteria, for I was wrought with outrageous fear, I expected more from the driver for the emergency we faced.

A wave of relief washed over me. We had arrived! Yet, as the vehicle stopped, it quickly dawned on me that I was in no shape to walk. It seemed probable that should I hop out of the ambulance's passenger side as though this were a normal car on a normal day, I would topple from the lightheadedness I was experiencing. I took the slightest moment to concentrate on my safe exit. As my feet hit the pavement I realized my balance was off and there was no sureness to my steps. I felt physically weak. I stumbled to a brick wall at the rear of the ambulance and sunk to my bottom, tipping my head downward as they pulled Evelyn's stretcher from the ambulance. A trauma surgeon ran to the medics, identified himself as such, and took over. A terrible, deep, black, incredibly awful thought struck me like a blow. I felt stricken with fright. The worst outcome hit me; had I not already been down on the ground, it would have dropped me.

"If I do not get up and kiss my Evelyn this moment, I may never have another chance while she is alive." I felt incapacitated. I was frightened. Terrified. My head spun with dizziness and I was unstable even sitting. I did the only thing that seemed potentially able to renew my strength in that instant. I called on the Lord for help in my time of trouble. In my head, with a fervent intensity and heartfelt mother's plea, I cried out in a silent, shouting prayer, "Jesus, help me run! Give me the strength to go to my Evelyn to kiss her one more time! Jesus, please help me run!"

I rose. I felt as though Jesus hoisted me to my feet and lifted my heart with hope. I ran a few steps to her moving stretcher and kissed my child's forehead. Thank you, Lord. That kiss gave me a bit of peace and the slightest sense of relief. Jesus met me outside the ambulance when I needed him most, and he spoke these profound words found in Scripture:

"At once [Jesus] spoke to them, "Take courage, it is I; do not be afraid."'
—Matthew 14:27

Chapter 4:

In the Trenches

I followed the stretcher a short distance through the Emergency Department to a trauma room that had been set up in preparation for Evelyn's arrival—a result of my friend Ashley's call from the yard. A trauma team was assembled. They were waiting for us. As we rapidly rounded the corner and I first laid eyes on them, I saw masses of men and women in scrubs, gloves, and masks. What struck me most was the manner with which they made eye contact with me. I instantly saw competent compassion. They were ready to save her life. I had done my part. I got Evelyn into the hands of capable medical professionals in a Level I Pediatric Trauma Center. I recognized the gift of the accident occurring near this fine hospital instead of in a rural area like the one where I was raised in central Illinois or in Robbie's southeastern Oklahoma small town. This accident in a location far from a major hospital would have changed the course of my family's life forever. We could have lost Evelyn.

A social worker approached me just outside the trauma room as the doctors and nurses began working to stabilize and prep Evelyn. I later saw in a restroom mirror that my kelly-green shirt, silver insulated vest, and white jeans were covered in my child's blood from her head wound. I'm certain the sight of me in that state only added to the gravity of the situation for onlookers. Social worker Emily Adler identified herself and asked, "What may I do for you? Do you need anything?" "I need a chair because I'm about to pass out. I need some water. I need a phone charger. (My battery had about 30 percent charge.) And, I need a rosary." Upon which my voice broke, and I added with a desperate emotional plea, searching the faces of those gathered nearby just outside the trauma room looking at me, "Does anyone have a rosary?!"

The workers set out to assemble the items I requested. I then turned back toward Evelyn, and counted twelve individuals in the room with her before something else diverted my attention. Days later, I learned from a nurse who was in the ER that afternoon that the following people were present: a trauma surgeon with two residents, three ER nurses, three respiratory therapists, an ER attending physician, a Pediatric Intensive Care Unit (PICU) nurse, a pharmacist, and an ER care assistant (thirteen medical professionals). Right outside the room stood a chaplain, an x-ray technician, a staff charge nurse, and a social worker. Everyone was tasked with meeting the needs of Evelyn and her family in the midst of a medical crisis. They were amazing. Children's Mercy has my respect and holds a special place in my grateful heart.

Once the doctors started ministering to Evelyn, my thoughts turned to Olivia, our teenager. The plan that Friday afternoon was for Robbie to pick up Olivia from high school to take her straight to a physical therapy appointment. Since Robbie drove to the hospital separately from me, I didn't know what plan, if any, had been made for picking up Olivia from school. Still a mom with mom responsibilities, crisis or not, I called her mobile phone and it went straight to voicemail. The time was 3:07 PM. High school dismisses at 3:10 PM, so her phone was on silent. I called again and again while watching them work on Evelyn, each time growing more and more anxious and distraught that I could not reach Olivia! I recall I had repeated the call eleven times before she called me, and we spoke. (To this day, I feel a bit of panic when I phone Olivia and she doesn't pick up the call. This is a trigger for me.)

I don't even remember what I said. I was extremely upset. Olivia later told me that my voice sounded foreign, unlike she had ever heard it before, void of any joy, and she knew in an instant that things were terribly wrong. She sought out her childhood friend and high-school classmate with whom she is the closest, Grace Hill, and shared the news with her track coach and a few teammates. Tears flowed. Prayers began. Meanwhile, Robbie had arranged for my mom, Mary Conlon, and my stepdad, Mike, to meet Olivia and take her to the hospital.

A few minutes passed before Robbie arrived in the Emergency Room. Amazingly, I had kept it together without crying until that point. Once I saw my spouse, I jumped up, pushed him into the chair I was using, collapsed sideways with his legs as my chair, threw my arms around his neck, and wept; deep, body-wrenching sobs of despair and pent-up emotion escaped. He wrapped his arms around my body and held me securely. I buried my face in his neck and hung on for dear life. I was so scared. I knew I was not in control of the situation with Evelyn and it was awful. Any terrible outcome was possible. Robbie held me and let me cry. We then dealt with some logistics with the social worker about handling the arrival of expected visitors: Fr. Storey, our pastor; friends Jane and Chris Hill; my dad, Tom, and stepmom, Jane; my mom, Mary; and my stepdad, Mike, with Olivia.

Shortly thereafter, we were whisked down the hall to CT imaging with Evelyn rolled along on a stretcher beside us. After the scan, we rode with her in an elevator and I asked how long it would be before we received any results. A man replied, "Uh, you should know something in about forty-five minutes." That got my attention in an upsetting way, and my instinct to be her advocate surfaced. "Then you must not be very concerned that there is bleeding in her brain." No sooner had I finished that sentence than the elevator doors opened, and I heard that they needed us in a parent-consult room to meet with a neurosurgeon before emergency neurosurgery. Those around us started moving quickly and with purpose.

We sat quietly with Jane and Chris in a small room as we briefly waited to meet the surgeon. Our dear friends comforted us with loving and supportive words, and Jane's embrace strengthened me. She suggested we pray and led us in prayer, and this slightly calmed my anxious heart. Dr. Christian Kaufman met privately with us and the Hills and composedly explained that head CT imaging showed Evelyn had suffered multiple skull fractures and required a craniotomy to relieve pressure on her brain from the large depressed fracture caused by the blunt-force trauma of the tree limb. He would have to saw all the way around the perimeter of the crushed, dented-in area of her skull, raise the section of bone, and secure it. He said the surgery would take two or three hours. He spoke about how the area of her brain below the depressed fracture controlled the motor cortex, and that she would have left-side weakness and decreased mobility from the injury. He had an even manner, and he came across as calm and capable without even a hint of arrogance. With that, he was off, and we were left to wait.

As we exited the room, we were told that our priest had arrived to bless Evelyn prior to surgery. He met us in the hall and said a prayer over our daughter as she was rolled swiftly toward the operating room. Robbie and I kissed her. The medical team whisked her away. Then the waiting began.

Robbie and I, along with our friends, both sets of my parents, Olivia, and Fr. Storey were led to the Ronald McDonald Family Room. Everyone was in a state of shock. Several other patients' family members were in the room, and due to the serious nature of Evelyn's injury and our heightened emotions, we were shown to a larger private waiting room. The nine of us sat around and attempted to remain calm. There were silent tears. It was tense, and each person was clearly trying to hold it together. Olivia was extremely distraught when she finally made her way into my arms. She saw the blood on my clothing and the worry on my brow, and her heart broke for her sister's uncertain situation. Olivia has a tender heart. She cried. Not delicate little tear trickles, but full-out, scared-to-death crying, and her body shook as I held her tightly. It was awful. Terrible. Dreadful. I couldn't make it better. I didn't lie and tell her everything would be okay because maybe it wouldn't be. Only God knew. Olivia asked if she could wear my vest, in part because hospitals are chilly, but deeply because wearing that article of clothing, with her sister's blood, would make her feel closer to Evelyn. Everyone was quiet and solemn. Not even Chris Hill attempted to break the tension with his ever-present wit. Always a gentleman, attempting to help in the only way he saw possible, he just kindly offered me water and snacks, which I declined.

We used our phones to update concerned friends and loved ones. My phone was blowing up with text messages so much that I finally handed it to Jane Hill and asked her if she would please help me by fielding responses. I simply couldn't. I didn't have it in me. I felt devoid of the ability to communicate about what was happening. I needed to be still with limited sensory input. It was just too much. My heart hurt. My emotional energy was spent. I offered silent prayers.

Not long after the surgery began, Robbie's friend from church, Doug Rivard, MD, Chairman of the Department of Radiology at CMH, found us in the waiting area and invited us to the radiology reading room to review Evelyn's head CT images. Talk about a God wink and God's design for our human relationships playing out at precisely the perfect moment in time—this was a tremendous gift to Robbie. Fearing the unknown is a difficult spot for a man like Robbie. As a physician, he has too much knowledge about potential complications and all the ways things could spiral downward or end horribly. Learning information and medical details about Evelyn's injury turned out to be calming, even more so for Robbie. Olivia joined us. Although Evelyn had suffered multiple skull fractures, her brain appeared to be somewhat okay. Evelyn had a normal CT scan of her cervical spine, which was a tremendous blessing; she was not paralyzed. The telltale signs of serious brain damage were not there, so Robbie was relieved. There were some serious unknowns, but we felt grateful that she had not sustained worse injuries.

The CT scan of Evelyn's head/brain, taken at 3:30 PM on April 20, yielded the following results, summarized by Robbie in a text that he shared with some of his relatives and close friends:

Evelyn was hit by a falling limb this afternoon. She has multiple skull fractures. She has a large depression fracture at the point of impact on the right side of her skull overlying her motor cortex that will be repaired in surgery. She has a fracture along the coronal suture that propagated into the orbital roof which is non-displaced. She has a lot of ecchymosis and edema from this around her left eye. She has a non-displaced fracture in the zygomatic arch. There is a fracture in the proximal portion of the mandible, which is also non-displaced. And she has a fracture where the internal carotid artery enters the skull. A CT angiogram shows no signs of damage to the artery. The CT scans also show a little soft tissue damage and very small areas of bleeding. It is a waiting game now.

Seeing 3D images of Evelyn's skull, which provided a visual of the indention that the limb had made on my child's skull, was pretty shocking. It sounds gruesome to share what went through my mind, but it seemed miraculous that her skull had not been split open by the weight and force of the fallen branch, killing her instantly.

I kept offering prayers of thanks to God for preserving Evelyn's life as we viewed images of the scans on the large computer monitor. It was the oddest sensation to see such terrible visuals of injury and harm, to know our little girl was at that moment "under the knife" to fix them, yet to feel peace and thankfulness that the outcome was not worse. I was grateful efforts were underway to repair the skull fracture. I believe the power of so many prayers shielded me from being incapacitated by fright in those early hours. Maybe my medical ignorance was also bliss. I think Robbie still had plenty to fear.

Those in the waiting room were truly shocked by the ghastly 3D CT head images we showed them upon our return. The point of impact was near the top and midway back to the crown on the right side of Evelyn's head. The section of her skull that was fractured and displaced was approximately two inches in diameter and depressed approximately one quarter of an inch against her brain. There was also a sharp shard of bone from the inner wall of her skull that appeared to be penetrating the brain. This could have terrible, long-term effects. When her skull absorbed the first shock of the blow, the force was so powerful it created a long fracture that ran from the depression on the right side along the coronal suture all the way around to the left side of her temple. Evelyn sustained left orbital roof and left lateral orbital wall fractures, as well as a fracture of the right condyle of the mandible, which is the part of the jawbone that hinges with the skull. Most worrisome, there appeared to be fractures in the bony canals in which the internal carotid artery, the main blood supply to the brain, runs. This understandably put the surgeons and my husband on high alert, for these fractures could create dire consequences.

We waited and waited. Tensions were high, and each person in the room handled it differently. My stepdad, Mike, is always relaxed and carries himself with a happy-go-lucky disposition. Little in life upsets that kind man. I'll never forget the deep worry and sorrow written in his blue eyes. Jane Niedzielski quietly approached me and said that her daughter, Melissa, was willing to drive over from Illinois to be supportive. In my state of mind, I only imagined a long and stressful drive for my stepsister, lacking the forethought to realize the emotional support and help Melissa could offer her mom as Jane stood in for me in my own home caring for the other children. I thanked Jane and said, "It's fine for Melissa to stay put for now," but I truly feel regretful over that knee-jerk reaction. I was beside myself on the inside, not thinking clearly. Later, during our period of waiting, I desperately wanted to sit quietly and soak up Robbie's strength by holding onto my stoic husband's arm. I felt leaden.

When Olivia returned from the cafeteria with Grandpa Mike, I learned she had had a meaningful encounter with a chaperone of volunteers who noticed her sorrow and the blood on her vest. She was a true angel among us when my daughter felt despair. "From the moment you came into the room, I knew something was not right. The social worker told me about your sister and I am very sorry. I don't know if you believe in God, but if you do, he has the power to help her get better and will help you and your family no matter the outcome." Olivia told me she smiled as tears filled her eyes, and she thanked the woman. Olivia believed this was a God wink. She told me, "I hope I'll never forget that woman's kind words."

Once we were notified that Evelyn was in recovery, we met with Dr. Kaufman again. He said he elevated her depression fracture and was pleased that nothing had lacerated her brain covering. She had very little venous bleeding. The elevated bone flap was secured with four permanent, small, titanium microplates, two shaped like dog bones, that would take six months for fusion and healing. A drain was placed under her scalp to decrease swelling. She had quite a scalp laceration, so he incorporated that into his surgical incision. She was left with four centimeters of what he called a dirty wound that would likely not heal the same as a surgical incision, and he would have to watch that wound closely. Evelyn did not suffer an intracranial brain hemorrhage. She had a tiny contusion, but nothing "sinister." However, it was in the motor cortex, so she would have left-side weakness, the extent of which was unknown. This sounded like a nebulous explanation.

Dr. Kaufman told us Evelyn had had seizure activity on the way to the hospital—this was news to us—so she was on Keppra, an anti-seizure medicine, for seven days. He said she had a low chance of developing true epilepsy, which was a relief to hear. However, my knowledge of the life-changing challenges patients with seizure disorder face caused fear of that complication to settle in the back of my mind. There was no damage to Evelyn's optic nerve; her sight would be fine. He mentioned the fracture through her carotid canal, which got Robbie's attention. At this time, there appeared to be no damage to the artery running through. Despite the focal blow to the top of her head, he did not see global brain injury that would prevent her from waking up. That awful possibility had not previously crossed my mind. I suspect the same was not true for my husband. She would still be intubated.

The Pediatric Intensive Care Unit physician would watch for signs of brain swelling overnight, and she would receive another scan if she was not behaving appropriately over the next twelve hours. We were in watch-and-wait mode. Dr. Kaufman said, "I think she'll do pretty well." Evelyn had lost some blood, and her hemoglobin was down to 8, with 11.9 g/dL as the normal lower limit of the range for her age and gender, but it was unlikely she would require a transfusion.

We felt relieved that the surgery was over. We appreciated the fairly positive report and thanked Dr. Kaufman. Everyone in our circle breathed a slight sigh of relief, but the journey had only just begun. When bad things happen, we shift into survival mode and we rarely think about the good that is yet to come. I believe that God does not waste anything difficult we experience in life, but I lacked the wherewithal to imagine future good while I was in the thicket.

"I will be with you always, even until the end of the world."
—Matthew 28:20 (CEV)

Chapter 5

A Father's Perspective
—Facing the Unfixable

My father, Tom Niedzielski, was an observer and participant at the accident that terrible afternoon, willing or not. I have tried to imagine my dad's horror. The fallen limb was so large. Evelyn was so small. She was badly hurt, but to a terrifyingly unknown extent. There was little any of us could do to improve the situation, desperate though we were. We were simply caught up in the momentum and forced to live through it, carried along roughly and erratically like driftwood in the strong, fast current of a river with rapids, never knowing what the next moment held. Evelyn's grandpa turned to his Heavenly Father and sought protective aid for all those impacted; Evelyn's body was fractured, but the hearts of the rest of us were crushed.

He wrote these words:

Julie had only taken a step or two when a tremendous "crack" focused our attention to a large tree in the back of the yard behind the privacy fence. A large limb high up on the trunk began to pivot downward and pull away from the main tree trunk. We could not see the limb hit the earth because of the privacy fence, but heard the terrible sounds of impact. Julie ran to the gate, much faster than I can move these days, and she wrestled with the latch trying to get the gate open. The gate was opened, and Julie, Jane, the others, and I ran to the place where Evelyn was under the smaller branches off the main limb. Evelyn had been hit by a large branch...hard. She lay in a pulled-up position holding Winston up close. Julie and Allie were trying to comfort Evelyn, recognizing the damage to her head was severe. I feared moving some part of the tree might cause additional damage to Evelyn, but was able to move branches away to allow some access to her.

I initially tried to make a 911 call on my cell flip phone but got an immediate response, "This call cannot be responded to, please call again." I did, with the same worthless response. Apparently, the fact that my service had been initiated in Springfield, Illinois, it tried to connect there, not in Prairie Village, Kansas. I yelled for someone else to try their phone.

Allie Goodman and my daughter Julie were holding and comforting my stricken granddaughter. I am good at fixing things. I found myself unable to fix what was before me. In my mind I said, "Oh God, please help Evelyn."

Winston had been moved down on Evelyn's legs and he had been hit by some part of the falling tree, with damage similar to Evelyn. He was wild-eyed and flailing. I carefully lifted him up and moved him off to the side, away from where Evelyn lay, and returned to a spot at Evelyn's feet. We needed paramedics to get hospital care for Evelyn rapidly. Someone indicated that a 911 call had been made and that Robbie had been alerted by Julie to the situation with Evelyn. He arrived quickly to see his daughter on the ground with massive head and foot injuries. Paramedics arrived and moved Evelyn away on a stretcher to the ambulance. Julie went to ride in the ambulance with Evelyn and the paramedics, and Robbie was to follow at some distance. Someone said for me to take Winston to a veterinarian's office and I asked, "Where?" since I did not know my way around Kansas City and did not get to the Goodmans' home in a vehicle. Allie said she would take Winston to a vet.

Jane and I knew we had to get back to the Overlease home on 93rd Street in order to get to the children left behind. We did not have a car. I was in anguish about the two young children alone at their home. Too many instances of one tragic incident quickly spiraling into an additional problem in a snowballing effect have been known. We could not let that happen.

We got out in front of the Goodmans' home and began running toward the Overlease home. Jane ran faster than I could. After a block or two, she was about half a block ahead of me, and was tiring. The city had a pick-up *day, and discarded items from most homes along the way were stacked up at the curb. People were free to pick these things up for their own use, and Jane waved down a lady in a car who had been getting things off the curb. That lady probably saw me, and Jane's panicked demeanor, and thought I was some kind of offender. Jane explained I was her husband with a bad leg, and that a terrible accident had severely damaged our granddaughter, and that we needed to get to the other grandchildren at their residence.*

The lady immediately started clearing the pieces she had picked up out of her car, made room for the two of us, and drove us to the Overlease home. We got to the children, Henry and Vivian, who were waiting on the porch. We explained that Evelyn had suffered an accident, and that their mom and dad had gone with her to the hospital. We said that we would learn more from them later.

Emily Finlason came to the house and said she would take care of the children. Mike and Mary Conlon contacted us, arrived with Olivia at the house, and said we could follow them to the hospital. We did.

Evelyn's own father, Robbie, wrote this:

I finished my morning clinic April 20 and had a follow-up with my primary-care physician. I had a blood clot in my right leg in January 2018 and learned through an ultrasound that it had completely cleared. It was a good start to Vivian's First Communion weekend.

On the way home I stopped at the Hallmark store in our neighborhood to pick up a card for Vivian's special day. As I was checking out, the sales clerk said I could choose a free card from a designated rack. None of the cards were all that great, and it took way more time to find one that I could use in the future than I had planned, but I finally found one and headed home.

When I arrived home Julie and her parents had Winston ready to go for a walk to pick up Evelyn at her friend's house. I prepared and ate my lunch, then changed out of my work clothes. Just as I had put my phone back in my pocket at 2:46 PM, a frantic call came from Julie. She said,

"A tree just fell on Evelyn, she is hurt, get here fast. Hurry!" "What?" I questioned. "Robbie, hurry!" she quickly shot back, sounding more terrified than I have ever heard her speak.

I immediately ran to my car without telling my younger kids I was leaving. As I was speeding up Delmar Street, my head was racing with thoughts of things that could be wrong. I was thinking of a broken arm or a broken leg. As I pulled up to the Goodmans' house, Jane Niedzielski was in the driveway waving me down, "They are in the backyard, Robbie! Hurry!" I have never before heard the kind of fear she had in her voice.

When I ran into the backyard the first thing I saw was a massive tree limb down on the ground. Julie was on the ground among the branches holding Evelyn's bloodied head, and her hands and vest were covered in blood. I was scanning the area to get a sense of what happened and what was transpiring before my eyes. I looked down to see Evelyn's bare feet, and the top of her right foot appeared to be flayed. The laceration was so large and deep I thought I was seeing the tendons of her foot.

I turned back and squatted down to Evelyn. She was screaming, and her right leg was kicking while her right arm was punching the air. Her right eye was fixed up and in. Her left eye was bruised and swollen shut. I yelled her name and pleaded with her to look at me. Her eye stayed fixed and all she could do was scream. I was trying to assess what was going on, trying to piece all of what I was seeing into a specific neurologic sign. My biggest fear was that her head injury was so severe that she had intracranial bleeding dangerously increasing intracranial pressure. Horrible thoughts were streaming through my mind, "Is she hemorrhaging? Does she have cortical blindness, and she can't see me? Is she in shock and scared and can't see, so she is fighting me off? Is she in danger of her brainstem herniating, which could cause catastrophic neurologic injury or imminent death? I have to do something to save her life, but I can't think of what to do. I can't let her die!"

Fortunately, the ambulance arrived shortly after I did. I told them to take her to CMH downtown. Luckily, Ashley was standing there, and I asked her to call ahead to let CMH know what happened and to be prepared.

Out of the corner of my eye I saw Winston's red leash. When I bent to pick it up I noticed Winston on the other side of the tree. He was rolling in the grass. I thought, "He is totally oblivious to the tragedy that is unfolding and is just playing in the grass." I ran over to get him. Uncharacteristically, he didn't try to run or avoid me. I picked him up and he was wriggling around, which he never does. Allie Goodman and Kelli Martin told me to give him to them so they could take him to the vet. "What?" I thought. "He just needs to go home." I put him on the ground to put on his leash. My hands were shaking and he was still squirming, and it seemed like it was taking forever to attach his leash. I am still not sure if I got it on or left it for Allie and Kelli.

Allie and Kelli were telling me to go. I sprinted to my car. I was trying to plug my phone into the charger and headphones so I could make calls on the way to the hospital when one of the EMTs walked over and said he knew it would be hard to resist, but I could not follow behind the ambulance. I said I understood and told them to just go.

They left and immediately turned in the opposite direction of the hospital. I instantly thought they misunderstood me and were taking her to CMH South, which wouldn't be equipped to deal with Evelyn's injuries. I pulled out and followed, fumbling with my phone to call Julie when a call came in from her telling me the ambulance driver told her that I could not follow or they wouldn't be able to drive "hot." I told her that I wouldn't and confirmed that they were going to the downtown hospital. I left them at 95th and Roe Avenue and turned to take another route.

As I was driving I frantically started calling the physicians I knew at CMH to make sure I had some familiar faces upon my arrival and to make sure the ER knew the severity of the injuries. The first person I called was my former pediatric ophthalmology attending, Scott Olitsky, MD. When he answered I immediately started telling him what I witnessed at the scene of the accident and started asking him questions about the neurosurgeons at CMH and if he was at the hospital. "Actually, I'm in Budapest right now," was his reply. I started apologizing, and as usual, he was gracious and told me he would send some texts to make sure someone would meet me when I got to the hospital.

I then called my friend Doug Rivard. I left him a rambling message similar to what I launched into with Scott. Next, I called my mother to let her know what happened, so she could immediately start praying for Evelyn. It was a lot tougher recounting the accident to her when I wasn't just talking in medical terms. I tried multiple times to contact my oldest daughter to let her know what was going on and to arrange a ride home for her. I never got through to her. After that, I called my medical practice partner, Bill White, MD, so he could notify the office staff and let everyone know what was happening. He is an oculoplastic surgeon and has seen and operated on many who have suffered head trauma and is more adept at neuro-ophthalmology than I am. He agreed that what I witnessed didn't follow any neuro-ophthalmic findings.

After I hung up with Bill, I was alone with my thoughts. My worst fear was that what I had witnessed was due to intracranial bleeding, or worse, brainstem herniation. "What if when I finally make it to the hospital Evelyn isn't alive?" I was trying to remember what my last encounter with her was like. Did we have a good morning together? Did I tell her I loved her before I left for work? "If I had gotten home earlier and Julie had left sooner, this may not have happened. Why did I waste so much time picking out an inconsequential greeting card? I have spent her entire life trying to keep her safe, and some random falling tree limb is going to take my little girl from me." I have never felt so helpless, so vulnerable, so devastated. All I could do was pray.

For some reason, I thought about Winston in that moment and how much Evelyn loves him and how much he loves her. Then it hit me. He wasn't just playing in the grass; he had neurologic injuries as well and couldn't stand up. What if he didn't survive? Or, if he did survive, but he had severe permanent injuries and we had to make the decision to euthanize him, what would we do? The thought was unbearable. Evelyn and the kids would be devastated to lose Winston.

When I finally arrived at the hospital I saw the parked ambulance. That surge of adrenaline hit me as only extreme fear can bring on. I parked and ran to the entrance. The security guard seemed to be deliberately moving as slowly as he could while checking in the people ahead of me. On the outside I was being as patient and calm as any visitor would be. On the inside, it was all I could do not to bolt past the security station. Finally, he got to me, checked my ID, and issued me my sticker. I told the front desk who I was, and a nurse immediately came out of one of the side doors and took me back.

I had been called in to CMH's ER so many times in the middle of the night during my ophthalmology residency for different types of injuries, but walking through the corridors trying to find my own daughter was a surreal and terrifying journey. When I rounded the corner to the trauma area I saw a room filled with doctors, nurses, and support staff. Julie was sitting down in front watching helplessly through the glass. When she turned around and saw me, she broke down and wept in my arms.

Shortly after I arrived, the on-call trauma fellow came out to talk to us. He said that Evelyn was stable, but would soon be taken for a head CT scan to see the extent of her head injuries. Although Evelyn was lying motionless on the table, I at least knew she was alive. My worst fear had been alleviated. I thought that no matter what came next, we could deal with it. She was stable and I hadn't lost her in route to the hospital.

They wheeled her out of the room and to the radiology suite for the CT. During her scan the CMH social worker took us and explained the sequence of events that were going to be taking place over the next few hours. Shortly after Evelyn left us, the trauma fellow found us and told us she had a large depressed skull fracture that needed to be repaired immediately. Although this wasn't great news, she was stable and apparently had no life-threatening injuries. My prayers had been answered.

In our conference with the neurosurgeon he informed us that a sharp bone fragment from the severe skull fracture looked like it could possibly have pierced the dura and caused brain trauma. He also informed us of the sizeable brain contusion of the right motor cortex underneath the skull fracture. This would in all likelihood result in weakness or even full paralysis of Evelyn's left arm and leg. And, although he was optimistic that as her brain healed she would slowly regain function of her left side, he couldn't be sure. She also had a contra coup injury to the left frontal lobe from her brain slamming into the opposite side of her skull from where the limb struck, and she could have some behavioral or even cognitive deficits.

Evelyn can run like the wind and has a freakish amount of endurance. I love watching her run. It seems so effortless to her. Without any training she can run faster and longer than most girls, and boys for that matter, her age. She is also smart and has a razor-sharp wit. How quickly our expectations change. I went from being so happy that my little girl was going to survive, to being devastated that she may never be able to run like that again or be "our Evelyn." All I could do was pray that God would continue to keep his hands on her through surgery and her recovery.

Fr. Storey was there and gave us all a big bear hug. It was 4:30 PM, and he had a five o'clock wedding to officiate that was considerably farther away than a thirty-minute drive at rush hour. I am not sure what traffic laws were broken to get him there and back on time, but his presence was a blessing. The Hills were there as well. I can never thank them enough for the comfort and solace they brought by arriving at the ER and staying by our sides the rest of the night. They were supportive through the entire ordeal. It is amazing the relief that is given when a friend is present to share your burden.

We weren't in the surgery waiting room for long when Doug showed up to take us to the radiology reading room so I could see the CT images. Luckily, the neuroradiologist who read the scans was still in the hospital to go over them with us.

The skull fracture was large, and it propagated along the entire left front coronal suture. She had multiple left orbital fractures, and the head of the right mandibular condyle was fractured. She even had a fracture of the foramen for the left internal carotid artery. Remarkably, none of these fractures, with exception of the large depressed skull fracture, were displaced. She had no fractures of her cervical spine. She had no significant intracranial or intraparenchymal bleeding. What a gift during a time of so many unknowns, when my mind was racing and conjuring up the worst, to now have peace of mind that the most devastating injuries had been avoided. She did have the contusions of the motor cortex and the frontal lobe, but we could deal with those. I will be forever grateful to Doug for taking the time to give us such peace.

After we returned to the waiting area my phone rang. It was the emergency veterinarian. He relayed to me that Winston was exhibiting signs of a vestibular injury, making it difficult to stand, but he too was stable. Again, his outcome was uncertain, but the vet was optimistic that, given Winston's young age (sixteen months old), he too would recover, maybe not fully, but most importantly, he would live. I thanked him for his call and his attention to detail. I updated him on Evelyn. He said his whole office was praying for Evelyn and not to worry about Winston. He would be well taken care of and he could stay there as long as we needed.

After a few hours the surgery was over and it was successful. The bone fragment that was a concern had not violated the dura. No vessels had been lacerated. Her skull had performed its job and protected her brain. Now the long road to recovery began. When we finally saw Evelyn for the first time she was unconscious and intubated. The right side of her head was shaved, but the nurses had cleaned her hair and given her two pretty braids that were connected at the back. Evelyn loves braids. Her left eye was bruised and swollen shut. She had a long sinuous incision in the area of her part on the right side. She had a large area of macerated skin in the area of impact. In a word, she looked beautiful. She was alive, and despite all that she had been through, all I could see was how beautiful she appeared to me.

It was a long night. Julie and I finally dozed off on a most uncomfortable couch, and in the middle of the night we heard the nurse say, "Well, hello there," to Evelyn.

Julie and I jumped up from the couch and went to Evelyn's bedside. Her right eye was open, looking at us intently. I immediately knew it was our Evelyn. She had fear and confusion in her eye, but it was Evelyn, all of Evelyn. I could tell she was confused as to where she was and why she was there. I explained to her that there had been an accident when she was at Macy's house with her friends. I explained to her what had happened and the injuries she sustained. She was staring at me sharply. I explained that she had had surgery to repair her head injury, and the tube in her mouth was to help her breathe. I told her that she was going to be okay. An enormous tear welled up and fell from her right eye as she shook her head, no. She knew she wasn't okay. She knew she was unable to move her left arm and left leg.

I have spent an obscene amount of money on Britax car seats for Evelyn and her siblings. I kept her in her five-point harness car seat, because she was small, much to her annoyance, long after her friends moved on to booster seats. I spent every weekend picking up sticks in our yard to prevent eye or other possible injuries. I, however, wasn't there to protect her from this tree. The hardest part of being a parent is realizing that I can't possibly protect her from everything she encounters in this life. All I can do is limit risk for her and pray that God continues to protect her with his loving hands.

"Trust in the LORD with all your heart and lean not on your own understanding." —Proverbs 3:5 (NIV)

Chapter 6

Emerging Post-Op into the Dark Night of the Unknown

Wen Evelyn came out of surgery sometime after 8:00 PM that evening, she was sent to the PICU to be monitored around-the-clock by a highly skilled nurse and multiple medical teams of specialist physicians. Robbie and I were extremely anxious to see her, but processing the magnitude of her injuries was also devastating. As we quietly entered the room, she was asleep in her hospital bed. Our child was intubated, a sad and instant reminder of the seriousness of her condition. I felt a wave of love wash over me, and I exhaled from the sense of relief I experienced from seeing our daughter again.

A sweet nurse had beautifully styled what remained of Evelyn's hair into a pretty side braid, and that side of her blonde head was our first view. Once we walked to the other side of her bed, we saw the sutures that closed the gashes on her shaved scalp. She had a thin drain tube coming out of her scalp, connected to a small plastic bladder that suctioned the bloody fluid discharge beneath her scalp to decrease swelling. Our sweet angel's face was in a state of quiet repose, but her head looked absolutely battered and quite gruesome. It was appalling and incomprehensible that our little girl's head should look so horrid. Evelyn's hair fell well below her shoulders before the accident. In the face of an emergent surgical situation Dr. Kaufman was forced to shave off a large area just off center on the top of Evelyn's head. The surgeon worked the scalp lacerations made by the limb into his planned surgical incisions, and the final shape of the incisions was a zig-zagging, misshapen, sort of wide and wild W.

A lot of her hair had been shaved, but the surgeon thoughtfully left hair around her temples and forehead to frame her face with just a tiny strip of long hair. That was a beautiful gift.

I was caught completely off guard later when a nurse handed me a plastic, gallon-sized, zip bag that contained Evelyn's bloody hair from the ER. It is hard to impart the emotions that surged through me in that moment. I felt deeply saddened. I felt disgusted and ill. I felt bewildered at the reality of our unexpected situation. Who possesses bags of bloody human hair? Yet I could not allow it to go into the trash. It was surreal. I kept it.

The section of Evelyn's skull that underwent surgery looked wicked— tremendously tender, raw, and painful. Evelyn's beautiful face was peaceful. Her color was good. Her left eye was still puffy and dark. However, it was the prettiest black eye I had ever seen. Aside from that, her face was unmarred. It was extremely sad to see that Evelyn had a breathing tube, and that would prove to be the root of one ugly stretch of brutal hours for our innocent daughter.

Evelyn was heavily medicated for pain on top of typical groggy sleepiness from anesthesia. The Hills, the Pepins (who kindly retrieved overnight essentials from our home prior to arriving at the hospital), and numerous relatives who were in the hospital during her surgery waited late into the evening and made their way two by two into the PICU room to see her. Evelyn's Uncle Anthony arrived from Dallas, as he already had a Friday night flight as Godfather to Vivian for the next day's sacrament. God wink. With six and a half years between us, my little brother has always been especially dear to me. It was a true blessing to have Anthony present the night of the accident. He held me in a tight embrace as I broke down sobbing in the waiting room. It was a moment no siblings want to share, but steadfast familial love soothes us during crises. As usual, Ant lightened the heavy mood of the room by relaying the story of how he couldn't gain entrance to visit without providing Evelyn's secret password, which he did not know. Chris Hill overheard Anthony's predicament, shared the code, "Trauma Massachusetts," and only then was my brother admitted.

I know seeing Evelyn intubated, not yet conscious, and in that injured state was exceptionally hard on everyone. My poor mom was reminded of my father's motorcycle accident in 1976, and she could barely stand to be in the hospital. She recalled the pain of my little brother's leukemia battle and his many weeks long in-patient hospitalizations when his blood counts failed to rebound after chemotherapy. The awful memories and fear hurt too much. She felt a desperate urge to get out of the hospital, and while she was there she was wracked with anxiety.

Robbie and I just kept staring at Evelyn, watching her intently, willing her to open her eyes until we could no longer keep our own eyes open or bodies upright in the wee hours of Saturday morning. Evelyn didn't stir. The waiting was agonizing.

Robbie and I were emotionally drained and nearing exhaustion. We decided to curl up together on the make-shift twin cushion to rest as best we could while Evelyn slept. I was so tired, but my brain would not shut off. My mind was racing, and I felt an awful combination of revved thinking and a total void of energy or peace. Robbie held me, and that was my only comfort. I have always felt so secure when held by my strong and loving husband. My mental state during those hours was such that I was no longer capable of formulating coherent prayers. I felt low. I positioned myself facing Evelyn's bed, and I frequently opened my eyes to check on her, watching hopefully for any sign that she was about to wake up.

At 2:45 AM, I heard the nurse say in a soft, sweet, welcoming and happy voice, "Well, hello, friend!" We leapt from our cot, bounded to the bedside, and leaned right in front of Evelyn's face. I wish she could remember that moment, because we were SO happy to see her! Her right eye was open. I was directly in front of her, and I grasped her hands in mine. Robbie was practically wrapped behind me, with his head right beside mine, in order to get as close to Evelyn as possible. She looked at us. We saw the spark of recognition and love. The way we humans communicate with our eyes is so remarkable. Then, heartbreakingly slowly, her eye filled with tears, and the tears began to run down her cheek. I know my eyes widened, my eyebrows rose, and I sincerely urged her to believe me, "You're okay! You're okay!" I insisted with a big smile. I meant it. I was immeasurably delighted to see her alert.

Evelyn has always been a straight shooter. She looked me in the eye, her appearance shifted in a flash to one of no nonsense, and she slowly shook her head as if to say, *Noooo*. According to her, she was NOT okay. Not one bit. Her expression said it all. "Do you hurt?" I quietly asked. With sadness on her face Evelyn gave me the slowest, slightest nod, *yes*. That made me want to cry, but I didn't. I was strong for my girl.

Her appearance shifted again, and she looked scared and confused, so uncertain and deeply troubled. Robbie has the gift with his deep voice and steady demeanor of instilling confidence in us when we, and his patients, need to lean on him. I always admire his ability to be calm, capable, and concise at the right moments, which is not my way. He said, "You've been involved in an accident. You had surgery, and you are in the hospital." Evelyn's tears kept running. We kissed her and smiled at her and reassured her that she was going to be okay. The nurse promised to give her medicine to help with her pain.

For the next ten hours, we felt like we were in the depths of hell. Understandably, Evelyn desperately wanted to talk, but she was unable to do so due to the ventilator. She was in a lot of head pain. She had eaten pizza for lunch before her emergency neuro-surgery. Saturday from 3 AM until 12:45 PM, she went through multiple rounds of vomiting while she was still intubated. It was dreadful. The tube that was placed in her stomach was narrow gauge, so suction efforts failed continuously due to clogs. It was an appalling, ugly, terribly awful mess. We would clean her, then she would vomit again. Her hair was soiled, which created a stench. It still had blood in it from the accident too. We couldn't wash it out thoroughly. It was just the saddest, most frustrating, and disgusting stretch of anguish for Evelyn. I feared she would aspirate each time she retched. We never thought it would take ten hours to wean her off the ventilator, but we all wanted to shout our praise from the rooftops once the nausea faded and she met the criteria to get rid of the vent.

The moment Evelyn could speak she didn't hold back. In rapid succession, she fired away statements and questions. "I have to go to the bathroom!" "What happened to me?" (Robbie told her.) "Why was I there?" (Initially, she didn't even remember being at Macy's house due to post-traumatic amnesia.) "Did I break anything?" ("Your head," her dad said.) "I'm sorry," she softly expressed with genuine regret; beyond her years in her practical and mature thinking, Evelyn was keenly aware of medical expenses after her little brother's surgery for a displaced broken arm after a playground mishap. We saw the wheels turning in her head. "When can I go home?" (We shrugged and sadly told her, "We don't know.") "When can I go back to school?" (Another shrug from us.) I told her that her best friend, Maggie, asked us to tell Evelyn that she loves her. "I love her too." That one caused my eyes to tear.

Feelings of total contentment and utter certainty that we still had our same Evelyn overcame us when we saw a lightbulb go off in her head and she unexpectedly commented, "Uhhh, I don't want to go back to school and [participate in an activity about which she often complained]." She said this with a big sigh and the full indignation, drama, and eye-rolling for which adolescents are stereotyped. In that instant, we were thrilled, for once, to see a flare of attitude. Robbie and I looked at each other, paused, then our laughter erupted and the smiles we exchanged spoke volumes. That was one of the most incredible moments of our time in the hospital. We laughed really hard, and in the midst of the struggle of Evelyn's first acute twenty-four hours after the accident, we felt hope and happiness. Evelyn showed us her spunky personality was indeed intact. We believed her fighting spirit would surface, and we knew that under the current circumstances it would serve her well. Those qualities count for more than people will ever realize. Hope on!

"And the God of all grace, who called you to his eternal glory in Christ, after you have suffered a little while, will himself restore you and make you strong, firm and steadfast." —1 Peter 5:10 (NIV)

Chapter 7

Evelyn had multiple medical issues that needed attention once she made it past the initial critical phase. At the time, I recognized that my thoughts were irrational, but I took the news of her right mandible fracture hard. Her greenstick fracture did not require surgery and appeared to be a minimal problem. That was great news. However, my heart broke when the oral maxillofacial surgeon said Evelyn had to eat foods of a mashed potato consistency for four weeks with soft foods for another two. It felt like that outcome added insult to injury. Truly! "Are you KIDDING ME?!" went through my mind. How was I supposed to provide adequate nutrition needed for brain healing with only mush to serve my little girl? I knew my strong-willed daughter would give me nothing but pushback about that diet.

As one would expect, Evelyn suffered a lot of pain from her head trauma. Think about how much it hurts to stub your toe, whack your funny bone, or miss the nail and strike your thumb instead. A thousand-pound tree limb crashed onto my twelve-year-old's head. Just take a moment to imagine the searing pain of having the thick bone of your skull dented by a tree. It is incomprehensible. She hurt. Her forehead throbbed, and she just wanted the pain to go away. It overwhelmed her.

Evelyn slept a lot during the day, but the nights were especially hard. She often awoke complaining of pain, sometimes describing the severity with words that were heartbreaking to hear. "I feel like there are weights on my head and foot," she shared as she broke down crying in exhaustion, unable to sleep in the dark of the night. In my experience, every problem feels magnified in the middle of the night, and that was true of Evelyn's agony. She tearfully told me how much she hurt, and she struggled during her entire hospital stay with extreme nausea. We were required to clean her scalp sutures and apply ointment daily. Her skin was raw and angry, yet we had to touch her tender, broken skin to tend her wounds to promote healing and prevent infection.

As parents, we were made weary from watching Evelyn endure awful pain. Her suffering was immense. Great worry accompanied this complicated situation, which was filled with many variables and worrisome unknowns. I was frightened about the potential of severe headaches becoming the new normal of my daughter's future. Would they go away, or was Evelyn's current state her future horrendous fate? I also worried about drug addiction from hospital narcotic use. Evelyn hurt! Her brain was bruised and irritated. At the very least she needed pain medications to take the edge off her ever-present agony so she could rest, heal, and recover. She was given morphine, Zofran, Toridol, oxycodone, Ibuprofen, and Tylenol, some by IV, but nothing worked to make her pain-free. She had to suffer through a straight catheterization to drain her distended bladder because she reported no ability to feel the sensation of needing to urinate. This also scared me, but we were reassured that it was likely a result of the narcotics. That procedure was painful and invasive, stripped her of bodily privacy, and I hated it for her. She was robbed of something as simple as being able to urinate independently behind a closed door. We take so many things for granted. So many times, I wished with my whole being that I could swap bodies with my little one and take over her hurting. Children should not have to suffer. It felt all wrong.

During our first two days in the hospital with Evelyn, Robbie and I only left her side to use a restroom down the hall, as there was no restroom in her PICU room. More than once Robbie started down the futile, "What if . . . ?" road. My husband contemplated the timing of the minutes he and my dad spent draining an old basketball goal base that they dragged to the curb for large-item pickup before Dad and I walked to the Goodmans' house. He asked himself if he should have called me on his way home as is typical for him, and I might have asked him to swing by the Goodmans to grab Evelyn, thus changing where our child was when the tree limb fell. He wondered if he could have possibly done anything, SOMETHING, to change the timing of our day to alter the outcome of the accident. He vented. I listened. I could tell he was grappling with a sort of unreasonable guilt over the accident, and I knew that type of thinking was useless and unfair to him. Finally, I said, "Robbie. That's not what happened. It was a terrible accident. It is not productive for you to ask, 'What if . . . ?'—so just stop. No good can come from that."

Robbie faced a comparable moment of truth days later in the hospital when someone suggested that we sue the homeowners. I was so proud of his character and so thankful that we were like minded and united in our belief about how to face the hardships and handle the situation. He said, "Unless we believe the Goodmans put a swing in their tree to deliberately injure their own children, this was just a terrible accident." I could not imagine the stress that would result from a lawsuit between families from the same school and church communities. The mere thought of it put my stomach in knots. We could tell the Goodmans felt incredible sadness that harm had come to Evelyn. We had no intention of trying to seek financial gain or bankrupt them over it.

We both experienced emotional anxiety—thoughts about how Evelyn's great health care, which was absolutely a blessing, came at a high financial price. These were normal thoughts for responsible parents, but our worry was compounded by fatigue. We knew the race before us was more marathon than sprint. It was more realistically a marathon with hurdles and sand traps tossed into the mix, but we could handle it together.

Throughout the day to a fluctuating degree, Evelyn's entire face swelled from IV fluids, significantly altering her appearance; then the puffiness faded. She slept a lot and preferred to rest on her left side, which was the one with the black eye from the fracture. This increased her swelling significantly. She hit the peak of swelling at the thirty-six-hour post-op mark, then after the fluid from her head ran clear and dry, her scalp drain tube was removed. The doctors told us that Evelyn's state of sleepiness was at a level that should be expected, given her injury and the major brain surgery that she experienced. Her tissue was healing.

The limb caused a gash on the top of Evelyn's foot. Amazingly, an x-ray revealed no fractures occurred. The plastic surgeon was initially concerned that a skin graft would be required. That would mean another operation and extended healing time, not an easy or pain-free road for Evelyn. However, in the PICU, the determination was made that a resident would close the wound right there in her hospital bed. She received medication to knock her out a bit, but she began writhing and moaning in pain when the lidocaine injections were administered to the top of her tender, ripped-open foot. The surgeon spent forty-five minutes sewing up Evelyn's diamond-shaped wound. He undermined the tissue on the inner wound edges, then began pulling the tissue together to approximate it from the lower layers up to the top. There were multiple layers of sutures. She ended up with thirty-five stitches in total.

Wound-care efforts began with ointment and a mummy-style gauze bandage, and Evelyn was fitted with a protective boot to supportively position her injured foot while she was weak in bed. Her foot looked painful, but she didn't often complain that it hurt. That always surprised me. I suppose that falls into the "everything is relative" category. Compared to a craniotomy and a bruised brain, a flesh wound felt like nothing to our hardy girl. It was the least of Evelyn's worries.

During hospitalization, Evelyn received services from Trauma, Neurosurgery, PICU, Oral Maxillofacial Surgery, Plastic Surgery, Rehabilitation Medicine (including Speech/Language Pathology, Occupational Therapy, Physical Therapy, Neuropsychology, and Nutrition), Wound Care, and Child Life. I attribute many of the significant gains made by Evelyn to the medical services provided by the dedicated, well-trained, and kind professionals at CMH. As a parent, I could barely keep up with the stream of nurses, physicians, and therapists who circulated through Evelyn's room to make sure her needs were met to the best of their ability.

Early on, my practical friend, Jane, delivered an attractive, floral, Anthropologie notebook to me. The doctors entering Evelyn's room quickly learned I must have it in hand with pen poised before they provided their assessments of Evelyn's progress. That notebook was key to helping me keep everything straight regarding my child's care and status.

Concerned people were naturally anxious to learn about Evelyn's status and improvements. In Evelyn's weak and sleepy state, it seemed as though we would have a great deal of downtime; the opposite was our reality. Evelyn could not feel sensation when touched or move her left arm, hand/fingers, leg, foot, toes. We were constantly busy in the hospital; simply helping Evelyn with pain management, bathroom needs, food and scalp wound care, eating (spoon-feeding her at first as she possessed no grip strength), therapies, and consultations consumed so much of our time that our initial communications with relatives and friends were minimal. I sent brief text messages as progress was made.

Eventually, I sent a couple of concise email messages that the recipients shared with other groups of people we know. This email was sent at 1:30 AM Sunday, April 22, when I finally had a moment to write to update close friends and loved ones:

- *Saturday positives: God is good.*
- *Both sets of my parents and my brother, Anthony Niedzielski; Robbie's mom and stepdad, Gwen and John Titsworth; Robbie's sister, Andrea Rogers; and Evelyn's dear 10-year-old cousin, Isabella, are in town. We are supported.*
- *Evelyn woke up enough for the ventilator to be removed. Huge change in her level of comfort.*
- *She could talk to us, communicate needs, and ask questions. She's appropriate/lucid. And still funny...*
- *Nausea/vomiting controlled.*
- *Foot wound was closed by a plastic surgeon without need for surgery/general anesthesia.*
- *Sunday goals—Keep temperature down. Hope to remove drain tube from neurosurgery. Hope to manage pain and improve neurological function. Hope she is able to eat soft foods. Due to her mandible fracture she'll be on soft-consistency foods a month. Evelyn's strong will is serving her well. We trust God's will.*
- *Love, Julie*

A close, longtime friend sent me one of the most remarkable, hopeful, comforting, and inspiring notes I have ever received on the morning of Sunday, April 22. She had been praying and reflecting on the previous two days, and God knew I needed an uplifting reminder about perspective after enduring such a treacherous and draining weekend.

Her words urged me to look at all the wonderfully positive things that were happening in our lives in the midst of our crisis and to remember to count blessings. People were coming together to comfort us in prayer with hopeful hearts. God spared Evelyn's life and was with her through her trials, fully at work in the difficult situation. "God is helping us and giving us the strength not to focus on the worst, but to believe God for the best. Although we know modern medicine has its limitations, we hold to the truth that God has no limitations and is certainly able to do immeasurably more," she offered. My friend implored me to turn away from doubt and despair, and instead, contemplate and cherish all the wonderful parts of my daughter's body that were working perfectly. I loved the solace I experienced as I took a moment to focus on each special blessing. Evelyn was Evelyn. She could breathe, see, and speak. Her broken bones were confined to her skull. Her carotid artery was not severed by the impact of the tree limb. So many blessings were apparent. Evelyn escaped spinal-cord injury and life-changing, massive brain damage. She was weak, but we anticipated improvement in her physical strength and mobility. My friend suggested Evelyn's personal health story could help reveal God's glory to others as he worked to heal her. Therefore, we chose to pray for the miracle of total healing. She closed her message with, *"Give thanks to the LORD, for he is good; his love endures forever"* —1 Chronicles 16:34 (NIV).

I desperately needed those words of trust and hope—a command to keep the faith. We were in the thick of it, and although the truth of her words rested in the recesses of my heart, I was not in a mentally contemplative place that allowed me to access those faith concepts. I was in a fog. Sometimes the best thing we can do for friends in need is to just show up. We may pray and ask the Holy Spirit to guide the message we offer, and he will take it from there. My friend's note shifted my perspective from that of sorrow to one of gladness. She reminded me to have an attitude of gratitude, a thankful heart.

Knowing many people longed for information on Evelyn's progress, this update was emailed at 11:46 AM Sunday, April 22:

> Hi—The neurosurgeon said the laceration area of the scalp incision is healing okay. Evelyn will have an MRI Monday for prognostic reasons. She will have physical-therapy and occupational-therapy consults to determine long-term outcomes. Her facial swelling around the eye with the orbital fracture is normal from fluids that mobilize from the scalp incisions. Her arterial line was removed. Her drainage tube from the scalp incisions was just removed. She will transfer out of PICU this afternoon. The current state of her sleepiness is at a level expected for her injury and the size of her major brain surgery.
>
> —Julie

Evelyn was visibly saddened by her inability to move her left arm during routine physical assessments of strength. It was not until the Monday afternoon following Evelyn's Friday accident that she first slightly curled her left fingers in and out. She could also tell which finger he was touching, which was an accomplishment. Likewise, we celebrated her ability to pivot her left foot and wiggle her toes to a small degree. The value of such skills, typically taken for granted by parents of healthy, active kids, became vitally important to her recovery. Everything is relative. In the prayers of our heart, we thanked God for each bit of progress.

Just like Evelyn's physical suffering, the fear I felt about her pain was gripping and relentless. Enduring pain was one of the greatest challenges she faced, and no one could predict how it would play out for her. It could be lasting, intense, and ugly. One day, I broke down in the hallway outside her room with a doctor on the Rehabilitative Medicine team over how hard it was to watch the suffering my child endured. The nurses had orders for various medications, but it was dreadful feeling that we were experimenting with approaches to alleviate her pain while she was not getting noticeable relief. It would be five days before they finally developed a pain-management plan that significantly eased Evelyn's intense pain with the miraculous combination of Ultram and Gabapentin at bedtime, suggested by Dr. Hartman. This also helped Evelyn get a better stretch of sleep. That was a noteworthy improvement to her condition, and it enhanced her recovery and our spirits tremendously. We felt immense gratitude.

Evelyn sincerely enjoyed the smile and easygoing manner of her favorite nurse, Katie. Katie helped me bathe my daughter in the shower in a special wheelchair, and it was as if she understood how vulnerable and shocked I felt watching my once fully capable and independent big girl switch to needing me as she once did as a baby. Evelyn was injured, pain-ridden, weak, and quite helpless.

Children's Mercy Hospital is an incredibly special place. I hope that none of you who are reading this will ever have to experience the care of the special people who work there, but if you do, I can't imagine a better place for such care. With their medical expertise and the hand of God at play, Evelyn was rescued from a terrible calamity. May God bless them and all pediatric hospitals for their important work. Hope on! Stay the course.

"Let us not grow tired of doing good, for in due time we shall reap our harvest, if we do not give up. So then, while we have the opportunity, let us do good to all. . . ." —Galatians 6:9–10

Chapter 8

A Healing Conversation

On the morning of Monday, April 23, I received a text message from Allie, the mother who hosted the group of sixth-grade friends the day of the accident. She said that she didn't want to intrude on our family, but she asked if we would allow her and John, her husband, to visit us briefly in Evelyn's hospital room that day around lunchtime. I responded, "Sure." I considered her request an incredible God wink. The Goodmans' twin boys, Mark and Mitchell, are in the same grade as our Olivia, so we have attended Curé of Ars Catholic School (Curé) together since our ninth graders were in kindergarten. The Goodmans' only daughter, Macy, is in Evelyn's grade at Curé too. However, Evelyn never played on any sports teams with Macy. It wasn't until sixth grade that the girls became friendlier and got together socially in a group. Robbie and I have attended many of the same Curé social events as the Goodmans over the years, but we are not in each other's close friend circles.

The three nights Robbie and I spent in the hospital room with Evelyn had been brutal in terms of her pain and suffering, despair over the magnitude of what she faced, and the lack of uninterrupted sleep for all of us. Additionally, I had been seriously struggling with the recurring thoughts of the moment of the accident, and those flashbacks attacked my peace of mind when I tried to catch some shut-eye. It was a vicious cycle. I had no appetite, and there were a million reasons why I couldn't relax and get adequate rest in the hospital. Lack of sleep and food caught up with us over time, and I, for one, faltered emotionally.

I say that Allie's request to stop by the hospital was a God wink, because she was someone who saw Evelyn up close and personal in the seconds after the limb struck her. Obviously, the accident threw us into a state of panic and anxious action in Allie's backyard. When I tried to think through every detail of what happened, there were some blank spots in my mental scene. I felt that if I could speak with Allie, she could possibly fill those gaps and somewhat ease my racing mind.

When Allie and John arrived in Evelyn's hospital room, they were clearly nervous. Dad and Jane were visiting Evelyn at that time. Allie and John took in the sight of Evelyn sleeping in her hospital bed. She looked tiny and fragile. They looked sad as they gazed upon her small, damaged body. I'm sure as parents with a daughter the same age, they were overwhelmed with empathy.

Allie and I embraced, and she began sobbing, apologizing for not keeping her composure as she had sworn to herself she would do. I asked her to step into the hallway with me. I explained my struggle with the repeating movie reel of the crack of the tree and rushing to help Evelyn. I told her I couldn't sleep at night, and I had no control of my vivid and troubling memories. We were both crying outside Evelyn's door.

I approached the nurse's station and pleadingly asked if there was a more private place where we could talk, an empty room or something. The nurse told me, "No." I was so upset that I wasn't even angry with her, just sort of shocked. I wouldn't give up. "Then is there a closet or anywhere at all semi-private where we may talk? We NEED to talk." She suggested I go around the corner where there was a short hallway that led to a couple of offices off the main corridor. We headed that way.

What happened next was a beautiful and healing experience. I told Allie that I wanted and needed to tell her the whole story of what happened in her backyard as I remembered it. I began. We cried. When we got to my account of the ambulance ride we actually laughed at times at the incredible outrage that I experienced at the driver's uncertainty about the fastest route to the hospital. She praised my lack of swearing. I told her about entering the ER and meeting the trauma team. I described our long wait during surgery and the torturous hours of longing for Evelyn to open her eyes for the first time after she was out of surgery in the PICU. I poured out my heart. I sobbed. Sometimes my body shook with anguish, and Allie hugged me and cried with me, truly understanding my heart as a mother since she too had seen Evelyn's glassy, unseeing eyes and her bloody head, and knew the situation was dire.

When I finished my story, I asked Allie to fill in some pieces that were missing for me. For instance, when I ran to the privacy fence that separated the driveway from the backyard where Evelyn lay fallen and injured, I peered through the fence slats, looked at the child on the ground, and I instantly knew it was her. However, in the hospital I could not remember for the life of me which top she wore. This was maddening. Allie knew. She remembered how pretty Evelyn looked in blue when they spoke at lunch. She helped clear the haze for me on other minutia that was lost in the major points of the catastrophe, but the details were missing puzzle pieces that I longed to place in the correct position to seek serenity.

I then asked Allie to tell me the whole story from her perspective, and we hashed through all of the details again. She told me what happened after I left in the ambulance with Evelyn. She described the immediate decision that she and Kelli made to seek emergency veterinary medical treatment for Winston because he was having seizures and unable to stand upright. His eyes were darting strangely, oddly exhibiting the same symptoms as Evelyn. They could not imagine Evelyn pulling through her accident and being forced to deal with the broken heart that would surely ensue should her beloved pet not survive. They couldn't stand by and do nothing to help him.

That is why they made the difficult parental decision to leave their daughters, Macy and Ava, at the house with the only other adult present, Ashley. Allie did not want to leave Macy, but they felt it was imperative to put our puppy in the position to have his life saved, if possible. That decision was fraught with parental guilt when Allie saw so much emotion on Macy's face as she grabbed a towel from the laundry room to wrap bloody Winston. Allie was distraught, but she had confidence that in the long run Macy would understand her actions; the Goodman and Martin families love their own dogs, too. Kelli quickly grabbed hands with the girls around the kitchen island, said a prayer for Evelyn, and prayed for Winston to recover so he could be there for Evelyn when she was out of the hospital. Allie described this flurry of action as "fast and furious."

Cushioned in a towel, Allie carefully handled nine-pound Winston in case he had sustained broken bones. Then, they raced from the house to get help. Allie cradled him on her lap and comforted our puppy as best she could as Kelli drove. They held hands. They cried. Allie said she never stopped talking to him, desperate to keep him awake and alert.

The women were understandably distraught and shaken by the event they had just witnessed, and Evelyn's condition was a big unknown. Trying to calm their breathing, they sped to a nearby vet, Mission Road Animal Clinic. "At the first vet we both lost it. It was just everything (that had happened)," Allie shared. They cried with the receptionist, who felt awful for them, while our puppy received blood draws and a sedative before heading to Mission Animal and Emergency Center on Johnson Drive, better equipped to handle serious animal injuries. They kept talking to Winston and told him he must stay alive for Evelyn. They prayed aloud for Evelyn and asked God to watch over both of them. Winston seemed to be in shock. The puppy had visited each veterinary clinic previously, so he was already in the medical records system at each office—God winks are apparently for dogs too.

Upon arrival, it appeared the clinic had positioned personnel out front to meet them, and this relieved the women. However, they quickly figured out the woman was just on a break, and that deflated Allie. Her comment to Kelli became colorful upon that realization. They rushed Winston inside. Since the other office had called ahead, the staff took him back for immediate assessment. Allie and Kelli were emotional as they attempted to communicate to the vet ER personnel the grave accident that had befallen Evelyn, the true seriousness of her apparent head trauma, and Winston's involvement in the freak accident. At that point, they did not know Evelyn's current condition or even if she had survived. They explained what they thought had happened because none of the adults were in the backyard to witness it. Allie knew that Evelyn had sheltered Winston from the major blow, because he was trapped in her arms when we reached them on the ground in the yard.

Allie and Kelli were in disbelief that it appeared that both Evelyn and Winston had suffered the same injury and showed the same symptoms.

While sobbing, they implored the doctor, "You must save this dog's life!" and told him he needed to do EVERYTHING in his power to help Winston recover so he could be there for Evelyn.

The veterinarian was calm and assured them that the puppy was in good hands. They left. Up to that point, as women on a mission, they had not received any information about Evelyn's status. Allie described her difficult and emotional return to her home where all the girls and many of their moms were gathered. Ashley received word that Evelyn was in neurosurgery, and that was a blow to Allie. They anxiously awaited status updates and prayed for Evelyn during her surgery.

Winston's condition and prognosis were additional painful question marks when Allie and I met three days after the accident. Kelli thought it was amazing and surreal that Allie would call for an update on Winston, learn of his progress, then turn around and Evelyn would have an almost identical report. Robbie and I felt immense gratitude for the measures our friends took. Allie wondered if people who did not have pets would judge the decisions she made after the accident. She decided it didn't matter because she had followed her gut. Even though it made her uncomfortable, Allie continued to call the vet's office to learn of Winston's progress.

Through all our sharing and crying we released a stress-inducing, pent-up, negative energy that we had both been mentally stewing on for days. It felt wonderful, freeing, liberating to talk to someone who really, truly understood the seriousness of the accident and the specifics of the emergency. We spent over an hour in the bend of that hallway, and those may have been the most therapeutic minutes that I experienced since the accident occurred. It sounds cliché, but I really felt as though a weight had been lifted from my shoulders when our conversation ended and we made our way back to Evelyn's room.

Allie and I shared a deeply troubling traumatic event. She helped me tend to Evelyn. She was by my side in the grass. Kelli dialed 911 and boldly summoned an ambulance after initially (and incorrectly) being told she had called a nonmedical line. Allie and Kelli saved our puppy. Those actions made a difference. We didn't seek it, but the events of April 20 connected us all in a life-changing way.

An excerpt from the book *Daring to Hope* by Katie Davis Majors was shared with me by my friend Shannon Lillis. In a simply beautiful chapter, "In the Thicket," I read, "God . . . will provide what we need, when we need it, even when we do not know what we need or that we need it." My friends met needs for our family, including saving Winston, that Robbie and I could not handle at the time. They blessed us. The quote went on, "God provides His Son, who meets you and provides grace for your gaps and light in your darkness." The author's words resonated with me when she described that we should always trust God and call our places of brokenness, pain, uncertainty, and difficulty: *The Lord Will Provide*. That truth moved me. I was intimately familiar with brokenness, pain, uncertainty, and difficulty after the accident, but yet, he provided.

Decades prior, God acted in my life. "Here is a stone," he said as he carefully placed one at my feet. "Now, here is another one," as he fit it perfectly beside the first one on the ground before me. On and on God went, the ultimate path paver, and he built the road of my life—stone by stone, tenderly, in his own time, and with loving wisdom—so that over time the foundation of my faith became solid. My loving family guided me in the faith. None of us ever fully arrive spiritually, but still, I was strengthened, loved, and equipped by him. By walking this custom path paved by our All-Knowing God, we met certain individuals, developed relationships, and it was all part of his plan. Great forces, outside the realm of our comprehension, were beautifully arranged to bless us. We were made ready for April 20 by the Lord Most High. As I reflected upon God's reminder of his deliberate, divine actions, my heart felt calm at the time when my inner journey in the midst of Evelyn's hospital stay was not easy. I was wrapped in God's warm love through prayer, support, and just the right comforting words from family and friends. I felt security and inner strength. I felt like a beloved child of God. I could "Hope on!"

Our friends are gifts from God. The people who crossed our path and walked through the times of despair with us were hand-selected by God because he provides. His beautiful promise is always there. It took tragedy and all semblance of normalcy in our family's life to be turned on its end for me to fully grasp the magnitude of God's power to provide.

In my mind's eye, I can just picture it. I imagine him being besieged by prayers to save Evelyn, and him smiling and slowly nodding his head. He knew. Our days are already written in the Book of Life. The prayers on the minds of all those kind people scattered throughout his creation were already within him, for he knows the depths of our hearts, our sincere desires, our needs, our petitions, our gratitude.

God knew he would spare Evelyn. It was not her time. Not yet. He knew the faithful would turn to him in my family's time of great need, would call out, and would draw closer to him through prayer. Prayers are our heartfelt conversations with our Almighty Father, and through our prayers we grow to know and love God more fully and with greater trust and hope. Who knew all that would follow when a tree limb fell on a young girl in a yard? God knew.

Blessing: For Courage
by John O'Donohue

When the light around you lessens
And your thoughts darken until
Your body feels fear turn
Cold as a stone inside,

When you find yourself bereft
Of any belief in yourself
And all you unknowingly
Leaned on has fallen,

When one voice commands
Your whole heart,
And it is raven dark,

Steady yourself and see
That it is your own thinking
That darkens your world,

Search and you will find
A diamond-thought of light,

Know that you are not alone
And that this darkness has purpose;

Gradually it will school your eyes
To find the one gift your life requires
Hidden within the night-corner.

Invoke the learning
Of every suffering
You have suffered.

Close your eyes.
Gather all the kindling
About your heart
To create one spark.
That is all you need
To nourish the flame
That will cleanse the dark
Of its weight of festered fear.

A new confidence will come alive
To urge you towards higher ground
Where your imagination
Will learn to engage difficulty
As its most rewarding threshold!

Chapter 9:

Traumatic Brain Injury (TBI) —Our New Lingo

The brain injury that Evelyn sustained from the blow to the top of her head was considered a Traumatic Brain Injury (TBI). The *Brain Injury Manual* that Children's Mercy Hospital provided states that while "more than 150,000 children are hospitalized with a brain injury each year, 20,000 of these children fall into the category of moderate to severe brain injury, with the potential for life-long issues related to the injury." Evelyn suffered a moderate to severe TBI. The process of recovery for those diagnosed is lengthy and complex, based on a multitude of factors specific to each patient. On Monday, April 23, Robbie and I consulted with Maria Korth, PhD, a neuropsychologist who really helped us grasp the scope of Evelyn's injury.

It reassured us to learn that patients such as our daughter, who are able to correctly follow commands within the first ten days after TBI, experience better overall recoveries. Evelyn suffered blows that impacted the frontal, temporal, and parietal lobes of her brain. The concern was how her learning would be affected going forward. Frontal lobe injuries may cause issues with the executive function skills associated with impulse control, forethought, reasoning, planning, and problem solving. Any parent of an adolescent will likely smirk upon contemplating the dilemma of distinguishing typical behavioral challenges associated with this age group with true difficulties from TBI as described. Parenting is never straightforward or easy. There is an expression in the medical field regarding "practicing medicine." I think it would be more appropriate for "practicing parenting" to be a common phrase.

We were told it worked to Evelyn's advantage that her pre-injury personality, behavior, and intelligence would play a part in her recovery advancements. Evelyn can be described as strong willed, hardworking, creative, and bright. Her dad jokes that she is almost as hardheaded as her mother. I take that as a compliment. She is a high achiever academically. However, kids like Evelyn are more likely to detect their intellectual deficits post-TBI than average students. Evelyn holds herself to high standards in all endeavors, so this could prove to be a challenge.

Dr. Korth told us that the recovery process for TBI is a long one, lasting six to twelve months. Additionally, research has shown the biggest factor in determining a patient's long-term outcome is the home environment. She said we, her parents, would have a profound effect on Evelyn's outcome. No pressure. She remarked that kids do well physically, and they are resilient. "You don't need to figure it all out right now," Dr. Korth said. She also encouraged us to allow Evelyn to make mistakes. We discussed how a crisis is a danger and an opportunity combined. We were advised to praise the effort that Evelyn put into recovering, not the daily outcomes. We must help Evelyn focus on her progress, with the ultimate goal of getting back to where she was before the accident.

Dr. Korth also reminded us that Evelyn has not had the same trauma experience that we have because she doesn't remember the event. She did not remember the accident or the first few days she spent in the PICU due to post-traumatic amnesia. She was not as traumatized as we were. We must gauge her emotional maturity and give her the details she requests with time. She reminded us that when Evelyn is tired, her skills will tank. She will be very sleepy for a while, then over the next several days she'll be more awake for visitors. This will wear her out, and she'll be exhausted. Dr. Korth closed with a reassuring, "I think she's going to do great."

On Tuesday, April 24, Evelyn met with Kelly from Occupational Therapy for the first time. Kelly's kind and easy manner enabled her to connect with Evelyn right away. Evelyn has the uncanny skill of being able to size up adults in a whipstitch. She can read people. Kelly passed Evelyn's test with flying colors. Ev sat on the bedside with a wooden board in front of her. The act of sitting upright was a major accomplishment, and she wasn't totally stable. Her task was to follow color and shape commands to grasp specific, raised, wooden peg handles; remove them from the board, which was similar to a toddler puzzle; and drop them in a discard area; then repeat the drill. Her hand moved like someone with the slow, uncoordinated movements secondary to intoxication, delayed and headed in an unintended direction. Her arm with open hand took a circuitous, slow-motion route to finally land on the correct peg. There was a clear disconnect and time delay between her brain's plan and the message that went to her hand.

Evelyn's exercise task was to raise her hands, one at a time, over her head. Doesn't that seem simple? The exercise was exceptionally difficult for her to accomplish, and this was upsetting to observe as parents. She was a healthy, agile, strong athlete mere days prior to the therapy sessions. We had our girl, alive and in one piece. We loved her no matter what. It took days before Evelyn was awake enough to participate in any therapy, yet that day had arrived. She had just set out on a long road to recovery with hidden obstacles lurking in the weeds.

"The journey of a thousand miles begins with one step." —Lao Tzu

"O Lord, my God, forever will I give you thanks." —Psalm 30:13

Chapter 10

The Depths of Our Unconditional Love

Our children are part of us. We marvel at them and love them with our whole being. As a little girl, I felt cherished by my doting mother. Her love gave me the comfort of a warm blanket on a cold day. She sacrificed for my good, loved me with all that she was, and instilled a sense of worth and self-confidence in me. She told me I was smart and beautiful and kind. To this day, as I am now a middle-aged woman, my father still closes our weekly Saturday morning phone conversations with the endearing words, "Take good care of Olivia, and Evelyn, and Henry, and Vivian. And, don't forget Robbie. Give them a squeeze from Grandpa. I love you. I'm proud of you." Dad was a cradle Catholic, so from that strong family tradition of the faith, my religious life was born. I am so grateful for love in my life and faith in my heart.

I fully recognize how blessed I am to feel confident in parental love and affection. Our parents' spouses, Mike Conlon, Jane Niedzielski, and John Titsworth, are three of the gentlest, most accepting, truly good-hearted people in our lives. James Robert, Robbie's brilliant father, committed himself to developing the whole person of Robbie during his upbringing: intellectually and physically. Grandma Gloria Overlease made sure the Catholic faith was part of Robbie's rearing, and his mom and stepdad further emphasized the importance of faith in God by living example. Gwen and John are wonderful people with deeply rooted Christian beliefs. More importantly, they use their faith to positively impact the lives of those around them in times of doubt or trouble through prayer and counsel.

My mother-in-law told me she abruptly ended her conversation with Robbie on his drive to the hospital as soon as she understood the severity of the accident and precarious status of Evelyn's medical situation. "Son, I've got to hang up right now and get John so we can start praying!" Gwen turns to prayer as her first line of defense, and she does it out of love and trust in God; that afternoon she experienced an urgency to pray.

Fr. Patrick Render, at our wedding Mass, told Robbie and me that we were only able to know love and love one another because our parents had first and sincerely loved us. We have been blessed exquisitely with God's love and the gift of fine parents. From love, more love flows forth; this is one of the most beautiful and awe-inspiring cycles in human existence.

It was my heart's desire to become a mother, and God blessed us each time we hoped and prayed to welcome new life into our family. Each baby was wanted with my whole heart, and we loved each child from the beginning, when two cells first became one. Our babies were made in love, and they are fully loved—unconditionally, no matter what. Women have the gift, the exquisite privilege, of growing new life within them. It is an amazing endeavor, so special with intricacies of embryology so complex, that it may only be orchestrated by an Infinite Being. The womb cradles the light of life, and each life is a gift from God. Our children are a treasure and proof of his love for us. I pray every person on Earth will choose to value and protect the dignity of human life from the moment of conception and Love All Babies—No Matter How Small.

Birth order is something that I've always heard about, but I never gave much thought until Robbie and I were the parents of four children and stereotypical birth-order characteristics became apparent. Sometimes, birth-order stereotypes and the ways they play out in families are practically laughable. Our children in birth order are Olivia, Evelyn, Henry, and Vivian. Each child has a special designation. Olivia is the oldest. Henry is the only boy. Vivian is the youngest, the "baby" of the family. Evelyn is our middle daughter. The middle position within a family unit is commonly seen as a difficult position, and I know that Evelyn agrees with that assessment.

The part that is funny for us is that Evelyn is more than outstanding in her own right. She follows an exceptional firstborn oldest sister. Three years separate the girls, yet that has never stopped Evelyn from striving to personally hold herself to whatever she considers to be Olivia's standard. Evelyn is her own toughest critic. Just as the youngest brother in a family of athletic boys will often find himself a fierce competitor among his peers for the sole reason that he has been forced to play harder and smarter to compete against his big brothers in sports, Evelyn's birth-order position and mental mindset have enabled her to make the most of the gifts she has received. She works hard. Her efforts are often supercharged. She cares about succeeding, and she's always up for a challenge.

That is all Ev. Her teacher PJ Palmer shared, "Evelyn is one of the most determined and driven girls I've ever had the pleasure to get to know." She has a force about her spirit that causes us to marvel at the grit of our young girl. She is pretty unstoppable, and we admire her for it. I also butt heads with her because of it, but I understand that is only because of our personality similarities.

Here's the thing: Robbie and I love each child because they are ours, part of us. We don't love them for the way they look, although we think they are wonderfully made, beautiful children. We don't love them for their report-card grades or test scores, although we celebrate their work ethic and academic accomplishments. We don't love them for what they have done on a stage, court, field, or track, even though we are their biggest fans and sincerely enjoy watching their activities. We simply love them. I believe every parent reading this fully understands our point of view. I hope every child reading my words will feel compelled to take them to heart.

There is a sweet children's picture book by Sam McBratney that we used to read to our little ones, called *You're All My Favorites*. The family of baby bears each felt their mother and father loved another bear cub the most. The message was about how very dear each bear was to the parents in their own right, and that they were all their favorites. Each bear was loved as a special and totally unique part of the family. I loved it. My children range in ages from eight to fifteen, yet they still articulate accusations that another sibling is loved more. At times, it feels as though there is no convincing them otherwise! Not until they become parents themselves will they get it. We have enough love in our hearts for however many children grace our family, and we love them individually, not in a comparative, greater or less than, sort of way. With Evelyn, in particular, as the middle daughter, I have struggled with getting her to understand deep within her being that she is loved without merit. She's not loved for how funny or smart or fast or pretty she is. She is loved because she is our dear Evelyn, the one and only.

Robbie and I heartbreakingly discussed this at her hospital bedside. Evelyn had a black eye, a swollen face, and a shaved head. She was not at the height of the social norm of physical beauty immediately following her accident, yet she remained strikingly gorgeous to us, and we loved her. She was playing soccer and running track in the spring, yet all of that came to a screeching halt when she injured her foot and brain. No longer could she perceive that she was loved for being scrappy on the field, scoring goals, or winning races. She was flat on her back in a hospital bed, unable to move her left arm or leg, unable to go to the bathroom, bathe, or eat without assistance. We loved her.

Her brain got struck and slammed into the opposite side of her skull by the tree's impact. She couldn't go back to school to finish her sixth-grade year. There would be no final report card documenting her strong work to allow her to earn kudos from her parents. We loved Evelyn with a rapid-firing brain or while she was in Traumatic Brain Injury recovery mode. We loved Evelyn from the moment we knew of her creation by God in my womb. We will love her until our dying day. Nothing she can do will make us love her more or less. This is so for each of our children.

This is how our Heavenly Father loves each of us. He created us in his image. He loves us. He is love. God's love for us is not merit-based or earned. We don't deserve it. It just IS. We are recipients of God's love through his grace. Through the misery of Evelyn's post-accident situation, I hope that one bright side to the event is that she felt genuinely loved every step of the way. Whatever factors she perceived as influencing our love for her were removed when the tree limb struck her. Time stopped, and from that day forward it is my deep, sincere hope that Evelyn will rest in the confidence and security of parental love that is real, true, and everlasting—with no strings attached. I hope this makes an impact on her heart for the rest of her long life.

"So faith, hope, love remain, these three; but the greatest of these is love."
—1 Corinthians 13:13

Chapter 11:

"Trauma Massachusetts"—
A Big Name for a Little Lady

After five days of struggling on my cell phone with slow, unskilled, one-fingered texting efforts to shed light on Evelyn's condition with others, I requested my laptop from home. I began to draft the following update on Wednesday, April 25, 2018, in the 7:00 AM hour. I wrote sporadically throughout the day when Evelyn drifted off to sleep, as she almost constantly needed my attention and assistance whenever she was awake. The update was completed in the evening, emailed to key points of contact (who further shared it), and posted to Facebook.

This was the first of several lengthy updates I wrote to share our story with a wider circle of relatives and friends. You have been privy to the whole, blow-by-blow story thus far. Many people we know outside of Kansas City read the note below as their first notification of Evelyn's accident. It shocked and saddened them. It also gave them hope. A grown man from our college days at The University of Tulsa texted Robbie stating he was shedding tears in an airport reading the news and imagining our horror. The next several chapters will allow you to step into our lives during April and May as I opened up and reached out through email updates, which were also posted to social media, to inform, share, and rejoice in Evelyn's healing and triumphs.

Dear Friends and Family and Prayer Warriors we don't know,

As I write to you, my sweet Evelyn is resting in her hospital bed. We arrived at the Emergency Room and were met by a trauma team on Friday, April 20, around 3:00 PM in the afternoon. At Children's

Mercy Hospital pediatric trauma patients are automatically, for security reasons, assigned a state in the US and a number, rather than traditionally identified with a first and last name. Our Evelyn became code name Trauma Massachusetts 3310. By the grace of God, my MD friend, Ashley Daly-Murphy, arrived at the scene of the accident and called ahead to request that a trauma team assemble. God wink. My 12-year-old's life was in jeopardy due to skull injury from a large fallen tree limb while embracing her miniature poodle puppy, Winston, in duck-and-cover position to protect him from the imminent blow. Evelyn's best friend saw the impact.

The backyard scene was of a horror I pray will leave me over time. I cannot thank Allie Goodman enough for helping me help Evelyn in the minutes after the accident in her backyard. She was on the ground by my side through the worst minutes of my life. Evelyn's head trauma and brain injury were significant, but her life was saved through immediate neurosurgery.

Winston was whisked away for medical treatment by mothers of Evelyn's friends present at the accident. Kelli Martin and Allie took him to Mission Road Animal Clinic, then due to the severity of his condition, on to Mission Animal Emergency where he was diagnosed with head trauma. He continues to improve. Those mothers knew the direness of the situation for our family pet, and they prioritized making an effort to save his life for the sake of Evelyn's future joy. I can't thank Sarah Parrish and many, many others enough for immediately asking for prayers for my child on our way to the hospital.

God is all-powerful! We are told in the gospel to bring our prayers to the Lord. You did that for my family, and we are immeasurably grateful. Ashley contacted me with the forethought to ask if I wanted Fr. Storey to meet us at the hospital, which I did. Thinking about that moves me so deeply. Evelyn's basketball coach, Tim Murphy, raced Father to the hospital, and Ashley arranged for a coworker friend to meet them to quickly escort him to us. He blessed Evelyn right before her emergency surgery, then they sped back to Curé with four minutes to spare for a 5:00 PM wedding! God's timing was perfect.

Emergency craniotomy to raise the depressed skull fracture to alleviate pressure on Evelyn's brain stabilized her. She went into the Pediatric Intensive Care Unit (PICU) where she remained (suffering in countless physical and emotional ways) until late Sunday. Our youngest child, Vivian, had her First Communion scheduled for Saturday morning, April 21, 2018, the morning after the accident, so relatives who live out of state were in Kansas City at the time of the accident. God provides. We have been surrounded with love and support. As the story has unfolded we have learned that there are easily thousands of people praying for us, not just in the US. Thank you.

In the ER prior to surgery, Fr. Storey assured us not to worry about First Communion. "Whatever you want. We'll make it happen." Little Vivian blessed my heart our first night in PICU post-op when I broke the news to her about a likely postponement of her long-awaited sacrament. I explained that Evelyn needed us to stay with her in the hospital. In her sweet and loving voice, she calmed my anxious heart with the words, "It's okay, Mommy. Whatever you think is best. I understand." Vivian is such a sweetheart. Her attitude blessed me.

Ev has multiple skull fractures and a fractured mandible. She must eat a soft diet for a month. Her right eye has been swollen shut from an orbital-roof bone fracture. She has 35 stitches in a foot laceration. Her scalp has a wickedly shaped line of sutures from the head laceration and neurosurgery. I told her she's going to have to be true to her confident nature and just rock the shaved-head look when she's around kids. Her scars are a badge of honor. Her shaved head is upsetting, but the hair will grow back.

Evelyn is an amazingly strong girl. She is determined, tenacious, motivated, intelligent, loving, faith filled, sensitive, courageous, beautiful, and goal oriented. If there is a kid in the world able to handle the outcome of this accident, it is our Evelyn. Even when the neurosurgeon described the potential for left-side paralysis due to the depressed skull fracture, I told Robbie, "She will be okay. If she wakes up, and the imaging results indicate she will never walk again, she'll say, 'Watch me!' She can do this. We will help her. I trust God." She has made amazing physical strides. She has been patient in affliction. She has been stoic and tolerant. I am so incredibly amazed by the grace with which my child has endured the last days.

We have had tremendous challenges in the hospital from the severity of her medical condition, but the care is excellent. She is in good medical hands, and she is held in the palm of God's loving hands. When we get discouraged by the extent of her suffering and feel disheartened, we persevere in faith. Robbie and I love her so much, and as the prayer of St. Francis reminds us, "When you cannot stand, He will carry you lovingly in his arms. Our Father will either shield you from suffering or give you the strength to bear it."

Today, Evelyn has a nasogastric tube to up her nutrition to build strength for brain healing. She can walk with minimal assistance. She can move her left arm and hand, which was not the case during post-op. She has her mental faculties, her humor, her old-soul wit that we so adore. She has an intact spinal cord. Her foot was not severed by the tree. It didn't break. Her seizures at the scene of the accident have not recurred. Her swollen-shut black eye (which I insisted looked like she played with eye shadow to create a "smokey eye," as she looked gorgeous right after brain surgery!) is now slightly open, allowing us to see both of her bright, beautiful, blue eyes. She has a lot of head pain, but we are working to control it.

She woke up with the request to turn on the lights, sit upright, and eat some peaches while watching TV. We have not turned on the TV once during our hospitalization until this morning, and she has had no appetite. She even had the spunk to request in my vulnerable moment to watch a movie that I have previously refused to allow her to see due to content. She's sharp. We were blessed to know a hospital physician with the ability to let Robbie see brain CT images during her surgery. The visuals were unreal. It seemed miraculous that her life was not instantly ended upon impact. I sat looking at image after image with immense gratitude to God and with thankfulness for the protection of her guardian angels. She is alive! Everything is going to be okay.

The outpouring of support actually makes me feel guilty. Thank you to Curé of Ars Catholic School, Christ Renews His Parish (CHRP) teams, religious orders, family near and far, friends, neighbors, Robbie's coworkers, and on and on. *Our hospital-room fridge is filled with roasted chicken, fresh fruit, hard-boiled eggs, and my dear friend's amazing homemade salsa! Love you, Jane Hill! I've taken the liberty of requesting breakfast hummus and lamb kabobs from my college roommate and still one of my best friends, Nada (Masri) Coleman, who learned to cook from her Syrian father.*

We have gifts like it is Christmas. God is all over the situation. So many people have been Jesus to us. I am constantly amazed at how the divine plan has been knitted together—a decade of building personal relationships and connections which came together in God's perfect timing to provide for our great needs during this crisis. My spiritual interior life has grown through my involvement over the last seven years in the Curé of Ars Catholic Scripture Study. I will forever feel indebted to Katie Axtell for sending an email that somehow circled to me, announcing the opportunity. My faith and connection to the faith-filled, multigenerational women in that study give me strength to lean on Jesus. To go through a traumatic event such as this without faith would be impossible. With God, all things are possible.

To our parents, our love for you is deep. We are so grateful for your help. You have swooped in to care for our other three children: Olivia (14), Henry (9), and Vivian (8) in a way that allows us to focus on our dear patient. Dad and Jane, thank you for staying in our home with the children while we are in the hospital. I know it can't be easy. Mom and Mike, thank you for taking the kids to their activities and on entertaining outings. To my in-laws, John and Gwen, thank you for driving Andrea (Robbie's sister) and Isabella to the hospital from Oklahoma to support us. John's sincere words to Robbie in the ICU gave us comfort with the message that our daughter was going to survive, be just fine, and go on to touch people's lives. "This is just going to be part of her story," John offered. Friends have been my disseminators of updates, and the prayers are storming heaven. We are so loved.

We are in a spot where our needs are well met. Everyone wants to feed us, and I have no appetite. Upon the departure of my parents from Kansas City, I will need assistance with meals. Your day will come;

I promise. For now, you may help us by doing small things with great love for someone not expecting it. Provide a random act of kindness for someone without expecting anything in return. In your heart, between you and God, please offer that gift on Evelyn's behalf. Be Jesus to one another.

Our close friends (you know who you are, and I fear in my sleep-deprived state I may not be trusted to list some without completely naming you all—to Jane, Becky, Emily, Katie, Ashley. . .I am deeply grateful) have met needs we didn't know existed, such as wide straws for protein shakes, a feather duvet for our hard sleeping spot, and soft toilet paper. A back massager surfaced from a gift box delivered by my longtime book-club friends when Evelyn had pain and needed distraction. Fun toys and putty in gift bags appeared as the occupational therapist entered the room to work with fine motor skills. Nutritious, protein-packed salads appeared when my lack of appetite turned to hunger, and I was fed. We feel your love. We couldn't go through this alone. Your support has meant the world to us.

To my rock, my beloved spouse, Robbie—you are the finest man I have ever known. It is such a blessing that you have the intelligence to "talk shop" with the medical professionals. We are under the care of countless teams and rehab therapists. I know how raw our emotions have been watching such suffering in our child over the last six days, but I wouldn't want to travel this rocky road with any partner but you. Your love for Evelyn is so boldly apparent as you lovingly watch her and help her in every way you are able. Her siblings have been understanding, empathetic, kind, and quiet (even her brother)—amazing, right?

As of this morning, Evelyn walked what turned into an amazingly shocking speed lap around the unit with the physical therapist. To leave she must eat substantial food volume by mouth, demonstrate strength and mobility that will keep her safe at home, and get the pain under control. We anticipate this will take three to five more days, but there is no crystal ball. She is motivated. Robbie and I spoke today, and he said, "I don't think the roller coaster is going to stop anytime soon, but I think the peaks and valleys are going to move closer together."

Please pray that Evelyn is able to tolerate eating soft foods, has decreased head pain, rests peacefully so her brain may heal, and continues to gain bodily strength for safe mobility. Instead of focusing on our doubts and fears about what the future holds, let us cast our eyes upon faith in action. This is an opportunity to pray like never before. It is a time to turn to God in total trust. Complete and utter trust. Jesus, I trust in you. I will close with something to remind us to laugh. I once saw a sign that read, "God never gives us more than we can take. Apparently, God thinks I'm a badass!"

Chapter 12

The Only Way Out Is Through...

⁓

• • • • • • • • • • • • • • *Thursday, April 26, 2018 Email Update:*
This was sent to a wide circle of family and friends:

When my little brother, Anthony, fought leukemia in 2000 I had a mental mantra that said, "The only way out is through. . ." I shared that philosophy with Evelyn today. This is such a wild ride. I'm wise enough to understand that I should expect this, yet it doesn't make the hard moments (or hours or nights) any easier.

Evelyn slept from 10:00 PM to 3:00 AM, which meant that I slept too. It was glorious! The next stretch of sleep was solid, and I climbed into Evelyn's hospital bed, snuggled up behind her under one of her new, ultra-soft blankets, and thanked God for my girl. It felt so good to hold her warm little body. The Trauma Team made their rounds just before 7:00 AM, and Evelyn downed a drink that provided pretty amazing nutrition in a small volume. She has to consume nearly 1500 calories and ~ 60g of protein each day on a soft diet while her mandible fracture heals. That is not a lot of fun. She was off and running, nearly a quarter of the way there after consuming one bottle.

At the suggestion of a physician friend who recognized that the monitors were not medically necessary given Evelyn's condition, I asked that she come off of them. One night after the monitors' alarms beeped, and beeped, and beeped. . . and BEEPED. . . AND BEEPED, I told the care assistant who entered to silence them, "That beeping is the devil." She quickly left wide-eyed and silent. Later, I took on full duty of some personal-care tasks that will be necessary for Evelyn at home, and we worked well together. Success. The next set of rounding doctors said that Evelyn was nearing the point from a clinical standpoint where she could go home, but she still wasn't eating enough.

She, like the rest of us, has highs and lows. She told me sadly, "I miss my puppy." I recalled that someone mentioned the slight possibility that Winston could visit in the hospital. The veterinarian at the animal hospital said he was gaining strength. I felt I had to convince Robbie about the possible benefit of our dog visiting the hospital. My husband may be the most practical person I have ever known, and the notion that I would suggest we arrange for a dog to go to a hospital could have been met with grave disapproval and a dismissive laugh. I thought Robbie would see the plan as utterly ridiculous, outrageous, of the "no way—not going to happen" vein, but he was on board. You see, we were often powerless to ease Evelyn's suffering. He knew Winston equaled joy to Evelyn, and that made the difference to her daddy.

Two of my friends were willing to do the "Puppy Transport" legwork, but first the request had to go up the ladder, through the appropriate channels, at CMH. Fingers were crossed. We received word from Child Life that "project reunion" was a go! Emily Finlason and her daughter, Josie, Evelyn's friend since they were babies, were visiting and helping us that day. Emily took off to the vet to pick up Winston. Later, with Evelyn in a wheelchair, we all met Emily and Winston outside, and the sun shone gloriously down upon us. The rays of sunlight fell upon us, warming not just our bodies, but also our hearts as we basked in joy from the light of God's gift of nature.

We hadn't been outside in a week. That thought had not occurred to me, so focused was I upon my child, until I felt the warm, splendid sunshine and was struck by the vivid brightness of afternoon outdoor light. It was marvelous.

I was so happy for Evelyn to see her little puppy friend. His wagging tail said it all. He was so excited his wiggles were almost too much for Ev! She could barely hold him, he appeared so crazed with excitement. It was such a happy moment. I was thrilled to cuddle Winston Bear, and I felt a sense of calm when his racing heart-rate eventually slowed as I nuzzled him against my chest. My sweet boy. I am so glad his young life was spared. I am so grateful that after all Evelyn was subjected to, she was not additionally forced to endure the loss of her adored puppy.

Later that afternoon during physical therapy, Evelyn walked through and out of the unit, took an elevator, then entered a PT room where she deftly maneuvered stairs, her task for that session. When she came out of surgery Friday night and awoke Saturday morning, Evelyn had left-side weakness, near paralysis—an inability to feel her arms or legs when they were touched or to move them at all. She could not move in bed. She could not feed herself, bathe, or go to the bathroom unassisted. For three days, we wondered if she would ever be able to normally move her left-side limbs again. We didn't know what the future held, physically, after her brain injury. We rejoiced at every slight indication that she was regaining sensation and the ability to move. It felt like a miracle to us when she stood for the first time or shuffled weakly across her hospital room.

Today, we were floored as we watched her quickly climb the stairs. To say that Evelyn is spunky is an understatement. She was told that she had to climb stairs in order to get out of the hospital; stairs fell into the "safe for discharge" requirement category. After she walked up and down the staircase, she looked at us with her eyes and face set in an expression that stated, "I can do this with ease. Is this all you're going to ask of me? Bring it on. I'm ready!" The physical therapist and I exchanged wide-eyed, astounded looks, and I broke into a mile-wide smile. PT cleared Evelyn for discharge. Amazing. Kids are incredibly resilient, especially physically. However, Evelyn's ability to transition from bedridden to stair climbing was joyously shocking.

In speech therapy, she was tasked with complex commands to test thinking. Her scores were reassuring to me that her Traumatic Brain Injury had not caused significant learning damage. With time, healing will occur.

The rehabilitation physician discussed a plan for pain management and outpatient therapy. The neurosurgeon who operated on her Friday said, "She looks great—doing very well." According to him, she's cleared for Friday discharge.

Evelyn got a great progress report from Occupational Therapy too. She used fine motor skills on a craft project. "I made a flowerpot. It looks like a preschooler did it, but I made it." She bounced a ball and caught it with her left hand. Again, just days ago, Robbie and I sat on the edge of our seat as OT and various physicians tested her grip strength. We celebrated a tiny movement of one finger on her left hand. They kept asking Evelyn, "Can you feel this?" as they touched her left arm for neurological checks every four hours after she emerged from surgery. She'd sadly shake her head, "No." It was heart wrenching. After a couple of days of this I wanted to scream at them to stop asking her that question! We prayed for hope in our time of despair.

Evelyn was exhausted by the end of all the therapy, and her mood and willingness to drink "disgusting and gross" protein drinks, as she coined them, reflected that. It was a difficult afternoon. An appointment with the nutritionist left me feeling discouraged about meeting future dietary requirements for the healing of Evelyn's brain and body. After hours passed, my confidence was restored. At the time, I felt so much worry, like her success rested solely upon my shoulders in my kitchen.

Robbie arrived after a full day of work while I was finishing what I quickly realized was a much-needed counseling session with a family psychologist. The accident was so awful that I've struggled with what I describe as a video reel that starts from the moment of the "CRACK" of the tree and proceeds through what was immeasurable fear and chaos at the scene of the accident. I told the whole story, sobbing and shaking at times, and I left with renewed confidence that I am experiencing a normal period of post-traumatic stress that will ease with time. I have a strong support network. I have faith in the Lord's holy will and divine plan to make good out of our trials. I have strong family, marital, and friend relationships to sustain me when I am weak. It may take time, but everything will be fine.

Robbie and I curled into bed with Evelyn, and I read aloud from a book given to Ev by my book-club friends. The best news of all is that my little dynamo, grumpy and belligerent as she was about meeting the nutritional goals, exceeded caloric intake by 8:30 PM. At one point, she was extremely emotional, and I pulled out a card booklet created by a classmate that she hadn't read yet because she had been so sleepy for so long. We belly laughed and broke the cycle of despair. "Think of something funny" is a grounding technique used to self-regulate emotions that was listed on a handout the counselor gave to me today. It worked. God love her. She did it. She drank the fluid because it is her job to get well. It didn't taste good. It made her feel ill. She was tired and wanted to go to sleep, but she did it anyway. That's the mindset necessary for a full recovery.

If she begins strong in the morning, then we are blowing this pop stand Friday! Please pray for a good night's rest and an appetite that will convince doctors that she's well enough to heal in her own home. Our whole lives were changed six days ago. What a difference a week makes. I will have to remind myself of the advice I gave Evelyn. When things are hard, we can't look too far into the future. Sometimes, we must look an hour ahead, and the only way out is through. . .

"I have the strength for everything through him who empowers me."
—Philippians 4:13

Chapter 13

Everyone Needs a Gorilla

I can't wrap my head around all that has transpired from Friday, April 20 at 2:46 PM to Friday morning, April 27 when we woke up in the hospital. First off, Evelyn and I had a restful night, which had become unheard of during our hospital stay. I crawled into her bed while she rested comfortably in the very early morning hours, snuggled under one of her new, plush and amazingly cozy blankets, and wrapped my arms around my child. I drifted off to sleep, and later, when Evelyn stirred, I said aloud, "Dear God, please help us accept your holy will. Please give Evelyn strength today, and give us the peace to understand your plan."

I have always joked that Vivian is my alarm clock. I seriously don't set one, as she enters my room and crawls into bed to snuggle me early in the 6 o'clock hour daily, often even on weekends. This routine had been replaced by a Trauma Surgery Team of five or six individuals entering our room to round on Evelyn at 6:30 AM while I was groggy, lacking proper undergarments, and had not yet brushed my teeth. Friday morning, April 27, the lead doctor was pleased that Evelyn had met her nutritional caloric and protein goals on Thursday, which did not happen without incredible strain between mother and child. Her nasogastric tube was hooked up to bags and provided nutrition as it ran from 6:00 PM until 9:00 AM. We were being threatened with leaving the hospital with the NG tube if Evelyn would not eat and drink more on her own during the day.

She was incredibly nauseous, and she insisted that every variety of advanced protein drink or "gross" hospital shake we offered tasted like "vomit." At one point, she received the boot-straps talk. My directive was,

"I understand that you don't like the taste of these drinks, but you must drink them anyway in order to get out of here. Think of it as medicine. We don't take it because we like the taste of it. We take it because we need it. Just drink it, Evelyn." She was an eight-ounce bottle short of meeting her daily goals, and the physician teams required two days of Evelyn demonstrating the ability to intake enough calories and protein to sustain herself to heal in order to be discharged.

So when we were told that Evelyn's success with nutrition on Thursday made the doctors ready to remove the NG tube for discharge later Friday, we were absolutely overjoyed. Evelyn was nervous about the procedure of the NG tube coming out. I was nervous for her. Sweet Mary Leonard of my Catholic Scripture Study brought the Eucharist to us on Sunday. It was moving for someone I respect so much to provide us with spiritual nourishment during a time of such tremendous sorrow and uncertainty. Mary has a peaceful nature and she is all things maternal. I love her, and her daughter, my dear friend Emily Claxton, who picked up protein-rich sandwiches and salad for us too. That Sunday afternoon, after a weekend in the PICU, Robbie pretty much insisted we take fifteen minutes to eat lunch together in a small private parent room down the hall while grandparents looked after Evelyn. I was resistant, as I hadn't left her. I didn't want to leave her. I felt so vulnerable after the accident that something would surely go terribly wrong should I leave Evelyn's side. As always, Robbie was right. He and I were able to share openly and in private over wonderful food about the challenges we were facing as parents. Our love for our child was so strong, and so many moments hurt our hearts so deeply in the hospital. It is appalling to watch the innocent suffer without means to end it for them.

On Sunday, Mary told me she left a small piece of the host/bread for Evelyn to receive. We, as Catholics, believe in the true presence of Jesus in the consecrated bread. Jesus is always in our hearts, but he was with us in a special physical way all those days in our hospital room when Evelyn was too weak to receive him. On the following Friday, a week after the accident, I shared with Evelyn that she would receive the strength that comes from the body of Christ before her nasogastric tube removal.

Evelyn is squeamish. The sight of blood makes her nauseous. She is often repulsed at things that fail to faze the rest of us family members. Evelyn thought the idea of the NG tube was disgusting and it physically hurt her throat. She complained that it felt sharp inside of her, and she was absolutely dreading and fearful about getting it pulled out, no matter how quick we promised the removal would be.

I sat on her hospital bed and said (thanks to help from an online resource), "Before he was given up to death, a death he freely accepted, he took bread and gave you thanks, he broke the bread, gave it to his disciples, and said: Take this, all of you, and eat it; this is my body which will be given up for you." She received the Eucharist and smiled. My soul felt peace.

While in the hospital, we received an outpouring of inspiring mes-sages, hospital survival items, and gifts. One family friend, Mike McGinnis, a fellow physician Robbie turned to for support during a trying health scare earlier in 2018, let Evelyn borrow a Michael the Archangel relic that came from a cave in Gargano, Italy, where St. Michael appeared. The handwritten letter said, "I cannot be certain of its authenticity, but feel it doesn't hurt to keep it close at times when burdens are heavy and faith can be challenged."

We were deeply touched by our friend's comforting words and will-ingness to share the relic, and I placed it in my fearful child's hand before the NG tube was pulled from her body. I prayed for strength for my child. I started a Hail Mary, the skilled nurse deftly pulled on the tube, and her little nose was normal again. In her next breath, Evelyn voiced readiness to get rid of her final IV. They obliged. Then, she was TUBELESS!!! It was a moment of bliss to know that she had lost her three IVs, one arterial line, ventilator tube, brain surgery fluid drain tube, gastric suction tube, and a nasogastric tube. Evelyn was no longer hooked to an unwieldy IV cart, and my heart rejoiced for her newfound freedom. I also experienced a pang of sad remembrance at my brother Anthony's hatred of his many tubes and rolling metal cart. Some sorrows never fade from memory.

The rest of the morning was filled with consults by Neuropsychology, Nutrition, Occupational Therapy, and Neurosurgery. Robbie and I have been together since he was an undergraduate engineering student way back in 1994. I was by Robbie's side through every single phase of the arduous medical training that ultimately, in 2008, finally led him into private ophthalmology practice. As the wife of a physician, I possess a real understanding of the commitment this profession demands. I broke down when I parted ways with Evelyn's neurosurgeon, Dr. Kaufman. I expressed my gratitude for every sacrifice he has made since he was a college student, including what I suspect are great sacrifices concerning time with his family now, to get him to the point where he was in a position to save my daughter's life on April 20. Words seemed inadequate to thank him for such an incredible gift. Dr. Kaufman was humble, and I admire and respect him for doing such important work for children.

With Casey, the Neuropsychologist intern, we discussed non-pharmacological ways to handle Ev's headaches and learned coping techniques to break the pain cycle. The psychologist told us about Post-Traumatic Growth, where in response to hardship people become more resilient. News of this phenomenon brought on a wave of emotion, as that is just the way my little daughter rolls. She is strong. She is brave. God has big things in store for my girl. In my heart of hearts, I know she will be okay.

Another bright moment came when nurse Katie asked for her pain score. Evelyn replied, "Nothing really hurts right now." That was a first. Praise be to God! I think my high point (which we often select and share daily during family dinner) was when Kelly, her amazing OT, mentioned that her eight-month-old baby girl was home sick, but she just HAD to come in to the hospital to square things away for Evelyn before her discharge. That mother's sacrifice for the good of my child in need deeply moved me. Evelyn loved her. Then, Kelly explained she had selected a special OT trained in muscular re-training for Evelyn's continued therapy, so that Evelyn might return to sports in a few months. When she told Evelyn that the best exercises she could do at home were planks and push-ups, I almost burst out laughing. I told Kelly that Evelyn was the Curé cross-country team plank champion, and there was confidence within me that with time, effort, and the help of professionals, we will get her back to her pre-tree self.

Going over the discharge paperwork was more entailed than anything I've previously experienced after a hospital stay. Evelyn looks so much better, but she will need a lot of tender loving care in the weeks ahead. It felt a bit overwhelming at times, and I hope I show up for each future medical appointment at the correct time and location! My concentration and memory have been failing me.

Thanks to the way our community came to our aid with snacks to nourish us, cards and signs to lift our hearts, fun and practical gifts, and creature comforts like real bed pillows and new blankets to make our hospital stay more bearable, we had a lot of packing to do.

We loaded our bags into multiple wagons. When we emerged outside, the day was all things bright and beautiful. I rolled her to a lovely spot by bedded flowers. Flowers are one of my great joys in life. She posed with her large cluster of shiny and bright balloons in her mandatory wheelchair. Passersby smiled and teased her to be careful not to float away. We were so incredibly happy to be going home. Our personal belongings and bags of gifts barely fit into Robbie's vehicle, and he's a packing master. We moved twice in one year, twice, during his medical training.

The drive home made me terribly nervous. My fear was paralyzing. I felt extremely worried about a car accident further harming Evelyn's brain, irrational as I knew the thought was. These feelings of vulnerability to possible accidents keep popping into my head, "intrusive thoughts" the psychologist called them. I squelched them halfway home and turned to see my little Evelyn slumped over asleep in the backseat under a swaying bouquet of helium balloons. She was practically hidden amidst her treasures. Life felt so wonderful. But, it got BETTER.

Evelyn's friends' moms organized quite a surprise for us as we turned onto our street. Across our yard stretched colorful, giant letters spelling, "WELCOME HOME EVELYN!" There was a big basketball sign, her new love, and even more surprises. The most noticeable one was that Evelyn's little brother, Henry, had dressed in his extra-special, inflatable gorilla costume for the homecoming. This was such an unexpected sight in our yard, yet so true to Henry's cute and wild character, that it was just the comic relief I needed at such a pivotal moment—our homecoming!

He rocked left to right on his legs, and moved his arms gorilla style. Vivian sat waving sweetly. Winston, recently picked up at our request by Allie for discharge from his own weeklong stay at the pet hospital, wagged his tail on the front bench with Grandma Jane and Grandpa Tom. I laughed and laughed at Henry, then I cried the happiest tears of joy! Someone (my Bible study leaders, Mary Leonard and Maureen Mancina, I later learned) even put brightly colored gerbera daisies in my front-step urns! They were so pretty. We were home! Evelyn survived. Life was okay again. Praise be to God.

Chapter 14

Community Makes All the Difference

Ｗe joined Curé of Ars Catholic Church when Olivia started kindergarten, and it changed our lives for the better. Nearly 700 students from preschool to eighth grade are enrolled at the parish school in Leawood, Kansas. After we moved into the Kenilworth subdivision in Prairie Village, Kansas, in January 2014, Curé became a six-minute walk from our home. It became the place where we worshiped, educated our children, volunteered, and developed a social network. We became deeply entrenched in the loving culture of the Curé family.

Through the Curé community I have developed the most meaningful friendships of my life. I have known some impressive and wonderful women over the last forty years, and many have touched me in lasting ways. Never before have I experienced the privilege of growing in faith among a true multitude of outstanding women. The parent volunteers in our church and school would be leading executives in corporate America if they chose to remain in the workforce. Instead, they commit tireless hours and boundless energy to the betterment of our church and school organizations without financial compensation. I have never met a more numerous or extraordinary group of smart, spiritual, kind, remarkable, and creative women. My church community is a joy and a true gift. Plus, it is one of the most significant blessings in my life that the mothers of my four children's favorite friends are women I not only respect and enjoy, but also truly admire and dearly love.

Ashley Murphy stood out to me and others as beyond impressive with her practically excessive volunteer leadership roles, professional life as a full-time pediatric hospitalist physician, wife, and involved mother of four. Our daughters, Evelyn and Lauryn, were born a day apart in 2006 before we knew one another. We became friends when we joined Mothers of Young Children when we both had three children, the youngest of which were baby boys. We grew in friendship in a playgroup with our rambunctious toddler sons, Henry and Brennan; then were pregnant and due a few weeks apart with our fourth babies, Vivian and Jamison. We have grown closer through the gift of time together for many years in Bible study, and I appreciate Ashley's mild, steady way. Not much ruffles her.

The following story, written by Ashley, demonstrates the layers of care and action that were happening in our circle of friends while Evelyn was fighting for her life. Ashley's presence was one of the tremendous God winks with which we were blessed moments after the accident when every minute mattered. In his omnipotence, God placed just the right mother of Evelyn's friends with just the right employer, a trauma-level children's hospital, in just the right place at the perfect time of day to make one phone call that sped up the process of our child's receiving immediate medical care. A skilled surgical team was ready, waiting, and prepared for Evelyn's arrival. Each day of our life has 1440 minutes, yet Ashley arrived at the scene of the calamity in the specific few minutes of that fateful day when her presence made an important impact. God's timing is incomprehensible. What follows is another account of April 20 from a key figure.

"Moments of Grace" by Ashley Daly-Murphy, MD
(written April 21, 2018)

How beautiful to have a group of about ten girls in my daughter Lauryn's class who get along and enjoy spending time with one another. How beautiful to have a mom who is beyond generous with opening her amazing home and enormous yard to the girls. It's nearing the end of the school year—closing in on First Communion for some, graduation for others, and about three weeks from the end of another busy, but successful school year.

We had a random Friday off school, so Allie Goodman generously invited the girls to hang out for a couple of hours. I had to run two of *my other children to their class auction parties, so the Goodmans' social opportunity was much better for Lauryn than being stuck at home, or worse…in the car with me.*

I dropped the girls off early and said I'd pick them up after grabbing my eight-year-old son from his party later. That afternoon, I arrived on Delmar Street and noted an ambulance on the street. My first thought was that an elderly neighbor had taken ill, but the scene didn't look urgent —no lights, no hustling. Then I noticed there were orange cones set up in front of the home where our girls were. I was going to give the mom trouble about what kind of drama happened—water in the basement or something else with new landscaping and construction (which had happened in the past and made for good laughs). At nearly the same time Lauryn called my cell. I answered with a giggly hello and was greeted with a momentary pause, followed by a shaky, "Mom."

At that moment, I knew something was very wrong. I told Lauryn I was there and to stay where she was. I noted the gate to the backyard was open and ran there. One mom was tearful on the phone and mouthed the words to me, "Thank goodness you're here; it's bad." I went farther and saw one of the girls was on a stretcher. She was sitting up, left leg bent in, left eye extremely swollen. She was making noises, saying it hurt. My initial assessment was, "OK, she's talking. That's good," but she looked as if that could be temporary. I was thinking, "Why are they not going right now?" I then noticed a furry immovable pile not far from the scene and the huge branch on the ground.

About this time, the ambulance driver was asking me for the address. Evelyn's mom, Julie, was in crisis mom mode, kind of jumping to attention and answering whatever questions were being thrown around. I told her she needed to go, we would handle things here, and to get on the ambulance with Evelyn now. I then called Children's Mercy Emergency Department and called in a trauma activation for a twelve-year-old girl with a traumatic head/brain injury from a falling tree. Two other moms were handling the dog, which turned out to be the furry pile near the branch, so I went inside to find the girls to talk to them.

I remember the girls kind of rushed me when I called for them. They were huddled in a back room, and I remember being thankful they were not watching what was happening outside. Evelyn's very best friend led the pack slightly and tearfully, and almost hysterically said, "I know she's dead, Mrs. Murphy, I know she is. That tree fell right on her and she wasn't moving." I was able to reassure them that Evelyn was talking by the time I got there. I'm not sure that did much to ease the stress and anxiety on the faces of the girls, but I could tell they needed an adult at that moment. A moment of grace. We then started to call all the girls' moms, who slowly arrived on the scene.

The moms arrived, stayed, prayed, and comforted the children. There were lots of hugs, tears, questions. Watching the day unfold was on the one hand profoundly traumatic, but on the other was profoundly humbling to watch this community of friends, families, mothers hold each other up and move forward. One mom pulled enough rosaries out of her car for everyone, and we immediately sat down to say a Rosary. During the Rosary, I contacted our parish priest with Julie's permission, and we were able to rush him to the hospital minutes before Evelyn went in for surgery. I work at the hospital, so was able to have one of my colleagues meet the priest at the doors and get him to the ICU just in time. We then returned him to church minutes before he was to celebrate a wedding as officiant. A moment of grace.

Another parent at our elementary school is a radiologist at Children's. I was able to call him, and although it was Friday after 5:00 PM, he had not left yet. He was able to review the film with the family and have a physician-to-physician conversation with Evelyn's father. A moment of grace.

The moms taking care of Winston, Evelyn's beloved puppy, were at the vet making decisions to save this furry companion who had similar injuries to Evelyn's. Their treatment and recovery journeys were remarkably and somewhat symbolically similar. Because in life there is never a convenient time for a crisis to occur, the host mother was also responsible for supplying dinner for her son's baseball team that night. I went into action, and we set up an assembly line to pack hot dogs, chips, and drinks. I called another mom from the baseball team who picked up the food to distribute to the team. That moment of assembly allowed the girls and their parents a time to smile a little, laugh a little, talk a little, and be there for each other at a tenuous time. The mothers talked about how we felt it was important to keep the girls together for a little bit so we would be updated at the same time and the girls could process things in their time, with each other, and with their moms in place.

I make it sound like it was all mom and their daughters rallying together. Make no mistake, though, for all the moms to be present and singularly focused on their daughter and the Overlease family, each dad received a phone call and with no hesitation picked up the rest of the Friday night responsibilities. The father of the family who was hosting was on his way to Hawaii for a business trip. I called him soon after speaking with the girls, before the Rosary, and was able to catch him with minutes to spare before he took off out of California. By God's grace, I was able to catch him. I reassured him that his wife, daughter, and sons were OK; but there was an accident in his yard and one of the girls was seriously injured. I could hear the wave of emotions on the other line—sorrow and fear for the young lady injured, longing to be there, a desire to support his family, the family affected, and to assess his property. He was stuck, though, and helped us figure out who to call to help with his boys, and made a plan for immediate return home once he arrived in Hawaii. He did in fact arrive in Hawaii and boarded a flight three hours later to come back to Kansas City.

My husband, Tim, was the maniac driver getting Fr. Storey to and from the hospital in about an hour, which included his time with the family (a twenty-five-minute drive on a good day, but this was Friday afternoon rush-hour traffic). My husband also happened to be Evelyn's basketball coach, a sport she was playing for the first time ever, as the team was limited on numbers, and she said she would join to fill in for the season. To say Evelyn took to the sport quickly would be an understatement. With her unique combination of grit, ferocity, and a little bit of sarcasm, she enjoyed the game, the competition, and the team camaraderie more than anyone expected. My husband, who enjoyed coaching Evelyn and getting to know her personality, and also the father of a daughter the same age, *was particularly empathetic to the severity of the trauma and what it must feel like to watch your fierce daughter fighting for her life, knowing there is nothing you can do but pray. He reached out to Evelyn's dad to let him know that although the women were all in a flutter managing the situation outside of the hospital, the men were more silently, but just as solidly, supporting him as a father and their family as friends.*

We all went home after a few hours, but then reconvened later at another home. We had some dinner and ice cream. The girls were able to just be together, and the moms were able to be together and talk through the evening on a more adult level. We were able to speak more candidly about our worries, our fear, the graces we witnessed. We were able to support the homeowner, who is a strong woman, but was clearly shocked and rocked by the events and was carrying a heavy burden of guilt and fear. We were able to get updates on Winston and John's return from Hawaii.

We were able to plan a little bit for the upcoming days. We talked with the school about the accident and the trauma our girls had experienced. We asked for support for them. They responded with immeasurable compassion, asking the sixth grade to attend Mass as a class on the following Monday to say prayers for Evelyn. Arrangements were made for the girls to spend a little time together at lunch to protect from the barrage of questions, and teachers vowed to keep a close eye on any signs they were distracted or upset.

As a pediatrician who cares for children, albeit not often critically ill children, I knew Evelyn's situation had the potential to be bad. Timing was critical. I wanted to be honest with the girls and the parents in a positive, but realistic way. Certainly, I was able to share more concerns with the mothers, the priest, and my husband than with the daughters. I was grateful that I could honestly tell the girls Evelyn was sitting up and talking when I saw her. I was the "expert" in the room they hesitantly wanted to seek answers from and believed in. I was able to talk them through what would happen when Evelyn went to the ER, had surgery, and went to the ICU. I was able to prepare them for the long recovery, what Evelyn might look like after the surgery, and what possible changes they could expect in the short term.

My daughter is a straight shooter. She asked pointed questions about the trauma and the recovery. There were tears and fear when she worked up the courage to actually verbalize what scared her. I was honest with her about why we should be hopeful, but also cautious about the outcome. I knew the girls would be talking at school and updating each other and Evelyn's peers, so I wanted the information to be clear, honest, but not scary.

The other component of trauma I am keenly aware of and was concerned about that night and going forward was for Evelyn's immediate family, of course—but also for the girls, who witnessed a horrific accident that hurt their dear friend. The images they saw could not, maybe ever, be erased and could haunt them for a long time. The same was true for the homeowners who are so wonderful about opening their home to any and all. The guilt any of those people could unnecessarily feel was on my mind: the "what if" questions, the looking for a different ending had one decision been made differently, the fear or guilt of "that could have been me." Those normal feelings are important to talk about and work through so that resilience abounds.

In light of these worries, beyond the control of any of us, we were left with the option to turn it all over to God in faith—with hope and trust in his will. He was with each of us in moments of grace.

"The steadfast love of the LORD never ceases; his mercies never come to an end; they are new every morning; great is your faithfulness."
—Lamentations 3:22–23 (ESV)

I admire Ashley and I feel deep gratitude to her. She serves those around her without ego, always humbly minimizing her significant contributions. She is an incredibly kind friend. Despite all her other commitments, she made sure I had hot coffee delivered to Evelyn's hospital room when I couldn't bear to leave my child's side to fetch a cup in those early days. Her understanding of the significance of Evelyn's medical condition and her continued efforts to check on me were thoughtful and touching. Ashley is stellar. She is a solid example of how God provided for us with love and grace throughout Evelyn's entire struggle.

The growth of our relationships with many families over the course of our four children attending school at Curé for over a decade led us to a place where, when Evelyn's accident occurred, we had developed a tremendous network of caring and supportive friends. With the participation of members of all our children's various sports teams, neighbors with kids at Curé in other grades, former playgroup moms, Mothers of Young Children prayer chain, Bible study, book-club friends, teams from Christ Renews His Parish, and the parents of children in our kids' grades, the entire school staff, and more, we had the force of a true prayer army offering petitions for Evelyn and our family. We were covered in heartfelt prayer, and our local group was just the tip of the iceberg. In retrospect, I attribute my trust and sense of peaceful acceptance of the situation to all of those powerful prayers.

Evelyn's friend and classmate Anne Rinella urgently told her mother, Jenny, what had happened to Evelyn. Jenny, a professor at Rockhurst University, shared the following with me: "A wide circle of Jesuit priests and colleagues from around the country continue to pray for Evelyn. I was with these dear friends when we heard about the accident. She is on the hearts and minds of many, being lifted in prayer."

With over 2,400 families in the parish, plenty of families have been in the unfortunate circumstance of needing prayer and other support as they have faced cancer, death, and a multitude of life lows. Evelyn has been in school with the same students since 4-year-old preschool, and there are three classes in her grade, roughly 70 students. Robbie and I were like deer in the headlights in those early days after the accident, and our dear friends stepped up and served our family through communicating with key school figures. This was a tremendous gift, as once they knew of Evelyn's condition, the floodgates were opened; prayers from all those young souls, school faculty, members of the parish, their families and friends were unleashed.

The day after Evelyn's accident, a track meet was scheduled for the Curé of Ars Catholic Youth Organization (CYO) team. Henry and Evelyn were going to miss that meet due to Vivian's First Communion conflict. However, Coach Janet McDaniel, mom of Evelyn's classmate Sophia shared the following report with us:

> *The girls wore pink wristbands that were originally created in honor of Jennifer Waldenmeyer, a former Curé mom and track and cross country coach who passed away after a long battle with cancer. The letters WWJD represented, "What Would Jennifer Do?" We felt Jennifer would tell us to rally as a team and pray for Evelyn, so that's what we did. We put on the wrist bands, held hands in a circle, and prayed together; then they ran their hearts out for their dear friend Evelyn. We were all worried and distraught, but we got it done. This is an amazing miracle with such a wonderful ending.*
> —*Janet*

An avid runner and a lovely person, Jennifer Waldenmeyer was an extremely positive and encouraging coach to my daughters. The wristbands gesture had great significance to us.

One of Evelyn's sixth-grade teachers, Mrs. Laura Wank, shared some of the details of what transpired at school on Monday, April 23, following Evelyn's Friday, April 20, accident. As I first read the teacher's description, my eyes filled with tears as I imagined the scene Mrs. Wank described. I was once a middle-school science teacher, and I could empathize with her. Teachers love their students, and receiving terrible news that involved a group of sixth-grade girls was a sad and challenging issue.

Mrs. Wank related:

> *My phone began ringing Friday evening and continued late into the night—descriptions of what had happened, what the medical game plan was or at least what it was at that moment, procedures and possible outcomes. We all talked back and forth about what we could do for Evelyn and her family and how to help Evelyn's friends through the school day on Monday. When my world is upside down I turn to my faith—having the*

sixth grade attend 8:15AM Mass on Monday was the first thought. When my class walked in Monday morning we all talked about Evelyn, what had happened, and what we could do— "write cards, send notes, buy her gifts"—"Yes, those are all great ideas, but the first thing we are going to do is turn to Our Lord for His help and guidance." We let Fr. Storey know our plan—so on Monday morning we proudly walked our quiet, reverent sixth graders to the front pews so that we could fully participate in Mass as a group of classmates united in faith and prayer. Fr. Storey announced to the congregation the purpose of our attendance. Evelyn's name was mentioned during the petitions and a special Hail Mary was said after Mass. My class lit a candle and said an additional Hail Mary. As crazy as it sounds, Evelyn's accident was a wonderful catalyst to talk about our faith and how it is important to turn to our faith in both good and bad times. We talked about friends and how special they are to us— "The best way to make a friend, be a friend, and keep a friend is to talk to that friend, and that is why it is so important to always talk to Our Lord." Wow, what a journey you all have had! I feel certain that Our Lord has special plans for his special Evelyn!!

Ms. Katie Lind, Olivia's former seventh-grade social studies teacher, shared a truly remarkable story. She was meeting with her friends one evening, and each was sharing work-related stories. One of her friends, a surgical nurse at CMH, recounted a recent neurosurgical operation involving a twelve-year-old girl who had suffered a terrible head injury from a falling tree limb. This nurse was in the operating room during the surgery and shared that she could feel the presence of God in the room. The patient was Evelyn! The nurse was unaware of Ms. Lind's connection to Evelyn. I was amazed when Ms. Lind shared her friend's experience with me.

About four months after the accident, I went to the first 8:15 AM Mass attended by the middle-school students in the new school year on Wednesday, August 22, 2018, for the Memorial of the Queenship of the Blessed Virgin Mary. I gazed upon the same group of Evelyn's classmates, now seventh graders, grouped in the pews once again. Tears streamed down my face during most of the Mass. The process of healing has been an emotional endeavor for me! I pictured them solemnly praying for the welfare of Evelyn when her medical status was still extremely uncertain on Monday, April 23. I thought about how scared the kids must have been, the concept of their own youthful invincibility shattered, and I was touched by the way they banded together to offer prayers to the Almighty. In Bishop Robert Barron's morning email for the daily Scripture reading, he reminded us, "We fight, of course, not with the puny weapons of the world, but with the weapons of the Spirit; by God we fight. So don't just honor and acknowledge the Queenship of Mary; get in her army." Amazing!

On the afternoon of Evelyn's accident, I repeated the first part of the Hail Mary aloud like a short chant as I held and comforted my pain-stricken little one. Later, when I called to mind the start of the Memorare of St. Bernard, "Remember, O most gracious Virgin Mary, that never was it known that anyone who fled to thy protection, implored thy help, or sought thy intercession, was left unaided," I felt overwhelmed with the gift of our loving mother Mary's involvement, her holy intercession, in my child's ultimate safety.

Each time I hear the words of the Memorare, I feel a profound sense of gratitude for Evelyn's outcome. I lived that prayer in a state of emergency. I implored her help! In retrospect, I feel a deep connection to Mary; it was as though she stepped in and participated in orchestrating the life-saving measures that blessed Evelyn. It is challenging to articulate, but it felt as if Mary had my back, for lack of a more eloquent way to express it. I believe God had a purpose in all that happened.

Sadly, I have known friends who have lost children, and my words fall short and fail miserably to recognize the deep sorrow of so personal a loss for those heartbroken parents. I can't comprehend why our prayers to save Evelyn were answered when similar desperate prayers of other mothers have not been answered according to their heart's desire. When I contemplate this mystery, for I have spent time pondering this matter in my heart, I simply don't know why. A friend offered, "God's ways are not our ways, and the mysterious ways of God baffle us." We must simply trust our Father in his omnipotence. He has a plan that has not been fully revealed to any of us in our inept human form.

Last year Fr. Storey adjusted the format of the weekly all-school Mass so that the stunning Memorare prayer is said while kneeling after Mass ends. It is remarkable that hundreds of children are learning such beautiful and comforting words, which they will carry in their hearts and minds throughout a lifetime. I pray that the seeds of faith will grow in this next generation of young people, and they will always lean on their faith and Jesus in times of trouble, fear, and doubt.

Memorare

Remember, O most gracious Virgin Mary,
that never was it known that anyone who fled to thy protection,
implored thy help, or sought thy intercession was left unaided.
Inspired by this confidence, I fly unto thee, O Virgin of virgins, my mother;
to thee do I come, before thee I stand, sinful and sorrowful.
O Mother of the word Incarnate,
despise not my petitions, but in thy mercy hear and answer me.
Amen.

The blessings that abounded extended past our church community. Olivia was significantly bolstered up by her Notre Dame de Sion high school community after Evelyn's accident.

Olivia wrote these words:

It might've been my friends that kept me sane. They looked after me and showed their support. Grace Hill would go on long walks with me and we would just talk. We didn't even necessarily talk about Ev; we just talked, and that was what took my mind off all the possible outcomes. My teachers were amazing. They checked in on me every chance they got and would continue to ask about Ev's recovery throughout the school year. Mrs. Paterson, my awesome biology teacher, even collected gifts from the freshman class for me to take home to Evelyn, and that really made her smile.

Our whole community served, prayed, and supported us with compassion and grace, true "boots on the ground" people of action. All the blessings we received flowed from the goodness of God through a fellowship of faithful Christians. Empathetic people in our midst kept us afloat by doing God's practical work to help us. We felt the love of God through his followers.

"Your every act should be done with love." —1 Corinthians 16:14

"[T]hat he may grant you in accord with the riches of his glory to be strengthened with power through his Spirit in the inner self, and that Christ may dwell in your hearts through faith; that you, rooted and grounded in love, may have strength to comprehend with all the holy ones what is the breadth and length and height and depth, and to know the love of Christ that surpasses knowledge, so that you may be filled with all the fullness of God." —Ephesians 3:16–19

Chapter 15

Friends with the Power to Change Us

My Friend Emily Finlason with a Servant's Heart

"Ev in ambulance. Huge tree fell and struck her head. Conscious but unresponsive, head bleeding, major eye swelling—pray!!!!!" Emily Finlason was the first one to respond to my 2:59 PM group text with, "Oh my goodness! Praying!" She was at Kansas City Christian at the end of her three kids' school day, having just read a birthday book for her son John Thomas's second-grade class. He turned eight years old two months after my Vivian's birthday. Emily swiftly gathered her children, left the building (no small feat for a woman of action as friendly and well-known for volunteerism on every school level), and drove straight to the front door of my home. That's Emily's nature. She has a servant's heart and she is a doer!

When Emily rang my doorbell, my stepmom, Jane, stepped out onto the porch, closed the door behind her, and practically collapsed into Emily's arms, crying in an exhausted embrace. My lovely friend and next-door neighbor, Alysia Quisenberry Carter, drove by my house that moment and saw the two women holding one another. Jane was overwhelmed by emotion from the magnitude of the serious injury and the desperation she witnessed at the scene of the accident, and by the unknown factors that existed regarding not just Evelyn's status, but her precious young life. When he was four years old, my stepmom's son, Mike Alexander, was hit by a car after he ran into the street while being picked up from his babysitter's house after his mom's workday, and Mike has lived with learning difficulties and an adult-onset seizure disorder. Jane understood our terror.

Evelyn's accident flooded all those terrible memories of a mother's worst nightmare to the forefront of Jane's mind. Emily held Jane and she wept. My father then made his way outside, and Emily described his face and affect as completely devoid of any energy or joy, simply bereft. My dad said, "I set up the cards to play Uno with Henry and Vivian." He then paused. When he spoke again, slowly and with hesitation, he quietly told them, "I don't know if I can play UNO right now." It pains me to imagine how powerless and unsure they felt.

After Evelyn's accident, Dad and Jane had to walk back to my home because nobody was available to drive them. The adults dispersed liked dropped marbles on a hard floor. I rode in the ambulance. Robbie followed me in his vehicle. Allie and Kelli took off with our puppy. Ashley stayed at the house with the seven remaining sixth-grade girls: Maggie Axtell, Anna Gillespie, Catherine Gyllenborg, Ava Martin, Lily Mason, Lauryn Murphy, and Macy Goodman.

Jane and Dad took off running the three-quarters of a mile from the Goodmans' yard to our house. Although they regularly work out at the gym and walk for exercise, they are not runners. After a spell, between the heightened emotions from the distress experienced at the accident, the anguish of reliving the memory from decades past when Jane's own son was badly injured, and the physical strain of running—Jane was near exhaustion. She flagged down a passing car and a woman stopped.

Jane desperately explained what had just transpired, shared the gravity of the situation, and offered an urgent plea for a ride for herself and her husband for the remaining distance to the home of her grandchildren whom were left home alone. Robbie had heard the intense distress in my voice when I called and had raced off without the kids.

Our city was scheduled for large-item pickup, an annual trash collection each spring, the following day. The woman who stopped to help Jane had been picking up "treasures" from the roadside where neighbors had deposited their discarded items, and her car was so full that there was no room for Jane and Dad to sit. Honestly. She had to hop out of the driver's seat and pull junk out of her car to toss to the roadside to make room for passengers to ride.

So, when Emily showed up at my front door, seeing a familiar face was a welcome sight to Jane, but she said, "I don't want to know!" I think Dad and Jane feared Evelyn hadn't survived the ride to the hospital, and that breaks my heart to imagine it. Emily told my parents that she was going to take Henry and Vivian home with her so they could go to the hospital. Since they live out of state and were unfamiliar with the route, she helped further by locating the hospital on a map. She sent them on their way and assumed the care of my children. That is how Emily operates.

When my childbirth labor on April 6, 2006, progressed to the point that baby number two, who turned out to be our sweet Evelyn, was going to arrive, Emily assumed care for my almost-three-year-old, Olivia. When Robbie and I moved to Oklahoma for a year for his glaucoma fellowship training when Olivia was three and Evelyn was one, Emily traveled down to Edmond and practically unpacked our entire house for us. When a trip to the pediatrician turned into a CT of the head that turned into emergency otolaryngology surgery for a retropharyngeal abscess for Olivia, Emily was there in prayer and person. When Henry broke his arm at age five at a park playground, Emily met me at the hospital and took my kids home with her. The gal should wear a cape! I need to stay out of hospitals! One mutual friend of ours Cori Cooper described Emily to another friend, "Emily has such a big heart. If there is a crisis, she's the first one to swoop in and save the day. She'd do anything for anyone."

Everyone deserves an Emily. Back in early 2004 she learned that the little house next door to their first home was going on the market. Emily and her husband, Mike, had a baby girl, Kenna Grace. Emily's faith is one of the main facets of her person, and she physically got down on her knees and prayed to the Lord for the new neighbor next door to be a stay-at-home mom with a little girl. Her prayer was answered when we moved into our home in June right before Robbie started his ophthalmology residency. I'll always remember the evening that Emily showed up on my doorstep with a big smile, a warm welcome, and fresh flowers and homemade cookies, which are two of my favorite things.

In those early years of our friendship as next-door neighbors, we took our babies for daily, long walks for fresh air and to lose baby weight, during which we learned about one another and grew in closeness. Emily felt like a sister to me. We took our little girls on adventures and chatted while they played in the backyard and dressed up as princesses in our homes. We understood the nuances of each other's marriages and family relationships, and with trust we talked and shared in ways that I always claimed saved our husbands hours and hours of listening time. Our lives and hearts were in a better state because we could confidentially vent. Together, we joined and attended wonderful Mothers of Preschoolers meetings, which helped us accept the truth that parenting is a journey, and support from friends makes it easier. As young mothers navigating the complex new world of parenting, our friendship has been validating —a tremendous blessing.

Through Emily's example, I learned many things that helped me grow as a person. Emily's faith has been central to her life, and she has spoken a lot over the years about various Bible studies she attended. Catholics were slow to join the Bible study bandwagon, so listening to the fellowship that Emily experienced from delving into the Word of God with fellow Christian women opened my heart to pursue the Catholic Scripture Study (CSS) opportunity years later when I learned about it. My experience with CSS has been paramount to the development and deepening of my faith and my internal peace. Without Emily's positive take on Bible studies and open sharing about her prayer life, I fear I would have remained stunted in spiritual growth. Although Emily was of a different Christian denomination, her influence had a profound impact on me as she demonstrated the soul-fueling norm of her weekly Bible study readings and meetings.

Her example made a mark on my life and enriched my family years later once I began growing in knowledge of Scripture and reflected upon its meaning in my life. The beautiful domino effect was that I then shared what I learned with my own family. My desire is that we will all grow in relationship with God, feel his love, experience his grace, and serve him, and our faith will be at the center of our identity—no matter the religion.

Emily loved me, her neighbor, but Emily casts a wide net over the term "neighbor." Through her example I learned to care for those around me, whether I knew them well or not, in their times of need. When a lady had a baby, Emily made a meal. When a friend had surgery or dealt with illness, Emily made a meal. Those generous favors flowed back to her a hundredfold during her mother's cancer illness and passing. Emily modeled doing small things with great love, as St. Teresa of Calcutta urges us to act. In my friend I had an amazing model of being a good neighbor.

A few people have shared with me that witnessing the prayer, tangible gifts, and support our family received after Evelyn's accident told them that some of it must have come as a result of the love and effort that we have provided to friends in their times of need. Those words warmed my heart and meant the world to me. Love begets love. There may be truth in their observation, but Emily has been a shining star of saintly support to countless individuals over the last fifteen years of our friendship. She set the example of being a loving servant to others. To know Emily is to love her, and I do.

$$\sim\!\!\!\infty\!\!\!\sim$$

"[S]erve one another through love." —Galatians 5:13

Saint Jane

It is safe to say that every person who knows Jane Hill is fond of her. She has a heart of gold. She is warm, soft-spoken, thoughtful, intelligent, and devoted. Jane is a wisp of a woman; a slight breeze could blow over her slight frame, yet she has a solid nature that instills confidence and shows her convictions and strength. She is always able to spin a bad situation to the bright side, a great quality to have in a confidant. Jane is a loyal, helpful, kindhearted friend. She's a true blessing to those around her, and she's my closest friend.

It is funny the way raising children with dear friends binds our hearts and lives in such meaningful ways. My oldest daughter, Olivia, and Jane's oldest child and only daughter, Grace, started kindergarten together at Curé. I met Jane on the first day of school in 2008 with toddler Evelyn and infant Henry in tow. My family had recently moved back to Prairie Village, Kansas, after a year spent in Edmond, Oklahoma, for Robbie's glaucoma fellowship. We were new to the Curé parish, and I was eager to meet other moms. Our sweet little girls became fast friends, and a lasting friendship among our families was born.

I admire Jane on many levels. She is a person of remarkable character. She leans on her faith, and she has faced her own set of challenges in life with grace. I trust God handpicked Jane as my friend. I want to ask you to think about how many people you know who have undergone any type of neurosurgery. I suspect, and hope, the number is small. Jane and Chris also have a son, August (Auggie), who was born in 2005 with a medical condition that required him to have a brain shunt when he was a few days old. Two years to the month prior to Evelyn's accident, Auggie's brain shunt failed. What presented like a viral illness was a medical crisis that rapidly spiraled into a near-death situation. Auggie's life was in jeopardy. Upon receiving the phone call, I sent out an urgent request for prayers via email before racing to the hospital. As parents and friends, we have been together when our children underwent emergency neurosurgery on separate occasions. We feared death was a real possibility, and that slams a parent's heart against the wall. It is hard to take.

How many mothers in any given city have experienced such a specific predicament with a child? I am confident that our friendship was divinely orchestrated to allow us to provide comfort and a deep sense of connection through our terrifying shared experiences. We have taken the same life-or-death ambulance ride with a beloved child, faced the ultimate uncertain outcome, and we have walked in each other's shoes. We have hugged and wept and prayed and rejoiced. Such things bind hearts.

I attended a women's retreat at Rockhurst High School in 2016, and the theme was, "Be devoted to one another in love," from Romans 12:10. That is a beautiful command, and the message applies to all our relationships. When Robbie and I were in the hospital with Evelyn, we were trying to get through one chunk of the day at a time. It was hard. We struggled to meet our basic human needs of sleep and nourishment during a time of crisis when our child needed us every minute. Thanks be to God and modern medicine, Evelyn had a proverbial parade of caregivers and therapists cycling through her room, and it was our aim to help them help her. We weren't concerned with our own needs for rest and sustenance. We ran on adrenaline and love. Our little girl's recovery was our priority.

That's where our friends came to our rescue. Jane swooped in to serve in her effective, yet quiet and gentle manner. She took care of us. She and Becky Pepin entered our home and, with the help of my stepmom, located the long list of personal and clothing items we requested be brought to the hospital. Only a close friend is granted permission to enter underwear drawers! Jane roasted chicken and vegetables, brought them to the hospital, and insisted we eat dinner. With the collaboration of Katie, our no-frills parent hospital cot spot was upgraded with fluffy pillows and a feather down duvet. I think my middle-of-the-night emails worried my friends, so they aimed to make me more comfortable so I would rest better. That love was medicine for our bodies and hearts. Love is all-powerful.

Jane is godmother to our youngest child, Vivian. Both families moved, and we now live around the corner from each other. We see each other all the time, walking our dogs or en route to and from school. Physical proximity only strengthens good friendships. Jane took charge of bringing Olivia to the hospital daily to visit Evelyn, and she made arrangements with my parents to take the two little siblings to visit their big sister too. Jane is that rare breed with the gift of knowing what to do to help and doing it without the recipient needing to ask. She provides the ultimate example of being Jesus to one another through her selfless nature. My debt to Jane is immeasurable.

Emergencies never occur at convenient times, so from the PICU we had to figure out the logistics of making sure Vivian was able to take part in individual and second-grade class photography, even though we decided to postpone her actual sacrament until the whole family could be present. Jane Hill, Olivia, and my stepmom, Jane, worked together to dress sweet Vivian in her special white dress and carefully styled and curled her hair under her veil. The caped crusaders swooped in and took charge. Sarah Parrish, my close friend and neighbor, thought to photograph Vivian with her daughter, Anna, Vivian's best friend. I could not take care of those matters, yet the important needs were met. The ancient proverb, "It takes a village to raise a child," is on the mark. I am ever grateful for my fellow villagers. They are the best. Even children were supportive to Vivian. Her classmates spoke to her at the church and promised to pray for Evelyn, and this comforted Vivian.

Jane Hill is an extraordinary person with a radiant soul. She inspires those around her to serve generously and with profound love. That love is of God. It is sent by God for our good. There is no doubt that on the journey of life, God can meet our every need. Through the imminent trials that arise we must take care of one another; we must help our friends along their path with devotion when their hearts are heavy and their steps are shaky.

*"A faithful friend is a sturdy shelter; he who finds one is a treasure.
A faithful friend is beyond price, no sum can balance his worth."*
—Sirach 6:14–15

God Is Extravagant in the Details

In Catholic Scripture Study at Curé of Ars, one of our leaders likes to remind us of important advice for our children to recognize: "If you hang around a barber shop long enough, you're going to end up with a haircut." We should aim to surround ourselves with fine people. Our multigenerational group of about twenty women spanning six decades is able to offer a lot of perspective from life experience. The three women who started this study in 1988, JoAnn LaBarge, Mary Leonard, and Maureen Mancina, are wonderful examples of good company. In partnership with God, they form a unique "Barbershop" Quartet. Through their dedication, they have fostered a nurturing and fulfilling spiritual environment for many women. We study sections of the Bible during the school year during weekly two-hour meetings, and the study is set up to cover the whole Bible over a five-year repeating cycle. We read notes prepared in the 1980s by the brilliant Sr. Marie Therese, and we independently answer daily questions that put us into the Word of God. During meetings, we share our answers and discussions ensue. Study members always take away "nuggets" of wisdom that we carry with us into the world.

In the middle of the night in January 2018, Robbie awoke with swelling and leg pain. He had developed a Deep Vein Thrombosis (DVT, blood clot) in his calf with clotting all the way into his upper thigh. It was bad. He was at risk of a pulmonary embolism (PE), which could result in serious complications or immediate death. The ER physician explained that there was no way to know which individuals may suffer a PE. Being young and healthy did not decrease Robbie's chances. If it happened, it was just bad luck. He started anticoagulant-medication therapy and continued going to work. For the first few days, each time he kissed me goodbye and left home to go to work, I wondered if I would ever see him again. I feared my beloved husband would drop dead, and I was terrified of losing him. It was awful.

I wrote to our faithful leaders and shared, "Sometimes I feel paralyzed by fear, and I pray for peace." Mother Superior, as we fondly refer to our witty and wise coleader, Maureen Mancina, responded to me with, "I know that this is VERY scary. It is the time to flip the switch to full trust, truly full trust. God is already at work." So often the Holy Spirit uses others to share a message, angels among us. Through her message, Maureen planted a little seed of faith and trust in my heart, and I carried it within until it bloomed after Evelyn's accident when I reflected upon it and strived to follow it.

I've heard it said that "God is extravagant in the details." He takes care of things in ways we could never orchestrate on our own. God is infinite in his wisdom. Maureen wrote in her final email to the Bible study group at the end of the spring cycle, "As we learn and grow through Scripture, we are continually wanting more in a relationship with Jesus, encouraging one another and helping where there is need. Our Bible study is not just a meeting but a bond in faith to live out the messages we learn as we go into the world around us."

Katie Axtell—Stealth Servant

Maureen's description could aptly apply to my friend Katie Axtell. She is a wife and mother of three, and her boy/girl twins, Grant and Maggie, are in Evelyn's grade at school. Maggie and Evelyn have been best friends since they were little. This is an exceptional blessing to me as Evelyn's mother because Katie is an incredible person. To Katie I credit my entrance into the Catholic Scripture Study seven years ago. We didn't know one another well when I received an email with news of open Bible study spots. She sent it to friends, and by the grace of God it was forwarded to me by a mutual acquaintance. At the time, I was a stay-at-home mother with Olivia in full-day elementary school, Evelyn in part-time preschool, and toddler Henry and baby Vivian at home. Life was busy. As strangers would often comment, I had my hands full. "Happily so!" I always responded with a bright smile. To participate in CSS, I needed two babysitting spots, and only five were available. God provided, and a new chapter in my life of faith and spiritual growth began.

Katie is a dynamo of a woman. She is outgoing, upbeat, hardworking, committed, smart, and active in her community. I have immense respect for the deliberate manner in which she seeks to grow in character in the ways that matter—faith, family, giving to those around her (whether the homeless or school families struggling through a crisis). Katie is "all in" when she decides to do something, and she is all heart. Evelyn refers to Mrs. Axtell as the "fun mom." Katie doesn't parent in a manner that seeks to be on a friend-to-friend level with her children and their friends. She is simply a happy, bubbly, energetic, cool, playful person. It is fun to be around her, and she comes up with exciting outings and activities that Evelyn absolutely loves. I once received an unexpected text photo of the friends before they headed to a roller-skating rink, skin and clothing alike, covered in glow-in-the-dark body paint. Katie is not afraid of a messy kitchen from a creative baking attempt. She even lets the girls concoct stink bombs and launch them from the tree house. She has taken the girls to haunted houses. This is not my way.

However, with Katie as my partner in adventure our combined seven children have experienced some pretty unique and amazing moments in life. Together, we braved an insane crowd of nearly 800,000 people in downtown Kansas City on November 1, 2015, to watch the Royals' victory parade after beating the Mets in the World Series. We snaked hand-in-hand, a train of ten humans, two of whom were terrified mothers, through the shoulder-to-shoulder crowd in the intimidatingly packed streets in front of Union Station without, by the grace of God, losing a child. With our minivans seemingly stuck for all eternity in traffic on a narrow road beside the WWI Monument and Museum, I nearly convinced Katie that we should leave them parked and walk the 8.7 miles home with eight kids.

We also procured, through no small effort, protective eclipse glasses and met up after driving north of Kansas City to get into the path of totality in Parkville, Missouri, on Monday, August 21, 2017, to give our children a mind-blowing view of a total solar eclipse. However, cloud cover at exactly the wrong moment ruined our view. It was a lesson in accepting that life does not always go as we wish. We share special memories. We have grown in closeness and understanding through our Bible study. Katie is a blessing to us, and she was absolutely an under-the-radar servant to my family after the accident.

After the accident, Katie was one of my friends who made a beeline to my heart through a couple of handwritten letters. She acknowledged the pain of our suffering and offered perspective on how to mentally contemplate and spiritually deal with it. There were times in the hospital when I was so exhausted and afraid and dejected from watching Evelyn's pain that I can liken it to drowning. I could have just let go, slipped beneath the surface, and into deep water. Katie was a lighted lifeboat with a cross on it. She listened and prayed and helped. She served. She blessed my heart.

Katie is also a bit of a stealth servant, and I love and respect her humble demeanor and quiet approach to helping. She, along with Ashley and Jane Hill, had the forethought to anticipate the importance of communicating with Principal Andrew Legler and Vice Principal Kim Hammers, teachers, and parents at the kids' schools on our behalf. Robbie and I were in survival mode, and my friends led the charge to inform the community of our needs and facilitated them in supporting us. Gift cards to eateries appeared in our mailbox. Ashley knew the importance of patients' visitors being limited to ensure privacy for proper rest and healing. She drafted a visitor guidelines document, and that was shared via email for the good of Evelyn's recovery. That task never would have crossed my mind, yet I believe it was a valuable communication.

Katie brought Maggie to the hospital to see Evelyn the Sunday evening she moved out of the PICU and into a room on a regular floor, two nights after the accident. It was a chaotic time. Evelyn's Uncle Anthony, my little brother, was getting ready to leave for Dallas, and Jane Hill had just arrived with my other three children for the first visit of Evelyn's two younger siblings. Ashley brought a wagon filled with gift bags from school families!

Evelyn was in so much pain that entire weekend that she was heavily medicated and experienced only very brief moments of being awake and slightly alert. She could barely move. Her head was a rather gruesome sight. The sutures zigzagged over her shaved head in Frankenstein style with purple marker still visible underneath from marks made prior to her operation. There were raw areas on her scalp, and her head looked quite battered and bruised. I knew the sight would be difficult for Maggie from my ten-year-old niece, Isabella's, emotional response to seeing Evelyn in her wounded state. Likewise, Henry was unexpectedly impacted by his first hospital visit.

I didn't recognize my sister because of her swollen, black eye. I felt sad and sorry for her when I saw her head. It was a super bad injury. I asked Mom if Ev knew her head was shaved, and I wondered if she would wake up and feel so sad when she felt she was bald on one side. I was scared and worried about her. She had a tube going into her nose and needles going into her arms. It made me know how serious it was. I just stood there staring at her.

Therefore, I prepared Katie in advance for what her daughter would witness.

Maggie handled seeing Evelyn in her weak and injured condition well. She quietly sat by Evelyn's hospital bed and provided supportive friendship through her loving presence. Then she bravely recounted for us what she saw in the Goodmans' backyard, because she was the only person present who was looking at Evelyn upon the impact of the tree limb. Evelyn's best friend was the sole eyewitness.

Robbie and I had accepted the situation as a terrible accident, but we wondered exactly what happened in the backyard when the tree split and fell on Evelyn. We saw a webbed tree swing on the ground in the grass in photos that were taken following the accident, which I requested from a mom at the Goodmans' home while in the ER to give the doctors insight. Because the privacy fence blocked the view of all the adults that day— and Evelyn remembered nothing—we had little information about the specifics of what had transpired.

Maggie shared her story, even though the accident was a traumatic event for her too. Her words gave us greater understanding, helping us process the situation. We learned of Evelyn's determined effort to protect Winston from the blow of the falling tree limb. Prior to Maggie's visit, we were in a state of, "How could this have happened?!" and, "Exactly what happened?" Evelyn's eyes were closed nearly the entire time of the Axtells' visit, but she opened them once, looked at her friend, and smiled. That was a beautiful moment, a gift for both girls.

Katie promised us that she and Maggie would be with us for the long haul, past hospital discharge and the staying-home-from-school recovery period. The girls' friendship remained strong during the summer months. They met at the city pool and went to the Axtells' club. They enjoyed sleepovers and met at the park to hit tennis balls. They giggled a lot, which was music to our ears as moms. Four months after the accident, Evelyn and Maggie started seventh grade. Miraculous! Our friends were true to their promise.

Maggie truly understands what happened to Evelyn to a degree greater than any other person present, including me. The friends have a special and lasting bond. Likewise, Katie listens when I need to share and vent. She understands my parental fears and vulnerabilities about something else harming Evelyn. She offers advice that God wants to take the stress to protect my children off my shoulders, and Katie reminds me to give it to him. She understands why I sometimes become flooded with emotion when something triggers difficult memories or when I simply feel overwhelmed with gratitude that my child is alive and not just surviving, but thriving.

On August 27, 2018, one week into the school year—and the day Dr. Alison Kaye performed an outpatient plastic surgery procedure of steroid injection into Evelyn's purple, bumpy foot scar—Katie and Maggie sent Evelyn a letter. I cannot read it without sobbing. Katie suggested, and I agree, that it will likely be the greatest gift my friend ever gives me. I am deeply appreciative for her beautiful letter, the frankness of her vivid descriptions of the sights and fears from that afternoon at the Goodmans', and for Katie's positive take on the experience. Her letter provides insight into another realm of the dark and light of April 20 and the journey that resulted.

Hi Evelyn!

Several months later, I'm finally making the time to write down the details that we remember from April 20—the day that you defeated the strength of that giant tree branch in Macy's backyard. You're already back in school for the 2018/2019 school year, running around the middle school hallways with your new shoes, new school supplies, and new teachers...but with the same friends who are so happy that you are there to join them. We felt inclined to tell you our whole story, even though some of the details may be repetitive with what others have shared. At least this way you'll have our complete perspective.

On Friday, April 20, you and a group of friends had the day off of school and had plans to see a movie followed by lunch at the Goodmans' house. Maggie called me on my cell phone that afternoon about fifteen minutes before I was supposed to leave and go pick her up from their home. Miraculously, I answered on the first ring since the phone was sitting on the counter arm's length from where I was unpacking groceries. I say "miraculously" because the silly phone is always in the bottom of my purse and I never seem to answer it on time. It shocked Maggie when I answered right away. She said, "Mom, you need to come and get me right away. Evelyn was in a terrible accident. A tree branch fell on her and an ambulance is coming to take her to the hospital." I could tell by the tone in her voice, this was a serious deal. Immediately, I rushed to the van to head over to the Goodmans' home.

Heading north on Roe Avenue from 95th Street, I passed your ambulance with your dad following in his car immediately behind. It was surreal to see; chills went up my spine. In trying to envision your injuries I thought you had probably broken several bones and were scratched up. I didn't realize you had head trauma at that point. I pulled into the Goodmans' driveway and saw Mrs. Murphy run through the back gate and start sifting through pieces of a tree branch in the backyard as if she was looking for something. I stepped out of the car, and Maggie came rushing out the front door and straight into my arms. She squeezed me so tight and she just sobbed, and sobbed, and sobbed, saying that "Evelyn was hurt so badly and I didn't know if she was going to be okay." As we just stood there hugging and crying, more moms of friends started arriving and people started going inside.

Ashley shared with me that a piece of the tree in the backyard had fallen and struck you in the head. She was calm as always (she's trained to be this way), but I could tell she thought this was serious. This was so alarming since Mrs. Murphy usually downplays most injuries (thanks to her perspective of working at a hospital). I called Mr. Axtell to tell him the news. When he found out that you were somewhat alert and resistant to the first responders when they strapped you to the gurney, he said very confidently, "It's okay, she's going to be just fine." He knew he had to be the calm voice of confidence for both Maggie and me.

By now there were mothers present for most of your friends that were there. Everyone gathered inside around the kitchen island crying, staring blankly, and retelling the incident over and over again from what they remembered. Everyone was in disbelief—as if this was a bad dream and it didn't really happen. We were uncertain if you were going to survive. In this moment we all knew the outcome of this was completely out of our control. What is there to do, but pray? I reached out to Maureen Mancina, who leads the Bible study group that your mom and I belong to, so she could circulate an immediate prayer request to our group. Mrs. Murphy contacted Fr. Storey, and I had heard that someone else had reached out to Mothers of Young Children (MOYC). Our school and church community already had their arms wrapped around you.

Mrs. Goodman and Mrs. Martin returned from taking Winston to the animal ER, and this was tough to see. Mrs. Goodman was inconsolable. This was the first time I saw her since the accident, since I wasn't there when it happened. I wrapped my arms around her in a hug, and she sobbed, and sobbed, and sobbed. The agony, pain, concern, terror, sadness, and guilt that somehow this was all her fault were all oozing out of her. She even commented that it may be easier to handle if this had happened to her own daughter. It broke my heart. About that time someone received a text update from your mom that you had arrived at the ER at CMH and were getting ready for emergency surgery to repair your skull. The doctors were preparing to save your life.

We brought ourselves to venture together as a group out into the backyard, so those of us who were not there during the accident could fully understand the story the girls were telling. If we saw the scene of the accident, maybe we could understand better the magnitude of the event. There, lying in the middle of the backyard, was more of a "hunk" of tree than a tree branch. There was a big branch, with lots of other branches coming off of it, and shards and shards of splintered tree bits—almost like someone had taken a sledgehammer to part of the tree branch. Attached to a section of the big branch was a web swing, tangled among the mass of branches. There was a pool of blood staining the ground, where you had to have laid in your mom's arms waiting for the ambulance to arrive. In awe of the size of the branch, I walked up to it to try to nudge it or move it a little to understand its weight. The branch was about the size of my torso, and leaning all of my weight into it, I could barely move the branch. It struck me then how hard the blow to your head must have been. I really started to worry. All the girls were telling their version of the story to try and make sense of it. Here is Maggie's version of the story—pieced together between sobs that first week, and through more calm conversations now that some time has passed.

Evelyn and I were standing in the yard side by side pushing Anna and Macy on the web swing, waiting for everyone's moms to pick them up. Lily was also standing next to us. Evelyn was holding Winston's leash in one hand and was pushing the swing with the other. Winston had arrived with Mrs. Overlease, who was there to pick up Evelyn and stopped to visit with Mrs. Goodman in the driveway.

We heard a loud crack and we could see that the tree branch that the swing was attached to was falling. The tree limb partially fell enough for the swing to hit the ground, at which point Anna and Macy jumped up and started running. At this point the limb was *still attached to the tree. Evelyn, Lily, and I turned to run toward the fence away from the house. Winston's leash wiggled free from Evelyn's hand, and he started running in the opposite direction from us (toward the house). Evelyn turned to go and retrieve Winston, and I turned to watch her. She scooped him up and started running back toward us, and then he wiggled out of her hands and started running in the opposite direction again! So she went to scoop him up a second time. By this time the tree branch started falling again.*

Evelyn saw that the tree branch was coming all the way down because she looked up just as it was a couple of feet above her head. She immediately ducked down to the ground with one arm over her head and the other around Winston, who was cradled against her stomach. It looked like the tree branch completely consumed her. It hit her head first and then fell on her whole body. The giant tree branch looked like it broke in half, maybe where it hit her head. She laid there shaking beneath it with one foot cut and bleeding, and her leg twitching. I said, "Evelyn, are you okay?" a couple of times and she didn't respond. I thought, "What do I do? I can't just stand here and do nothing!"

Then Mrs. Overlease came rushing into the backyard and everything was crazy. She knelt on the ground holding Evelyn. Mrs. Goodman was trying to help Mrs. Overlease and was trying to get Winston free from Evelyn's grip. Mrs. Martin called an ambulance and rushed all of us girls inside away from the craziness, shouting, "Go inside, girls. You don't need to see all of this!" I tried to wash out my eyes of the terrible scene. I peeked outside—bad idea. I saw my best friend screaming and trembling as if it was the worst pain in the world, and it probably was. I couldn't imagine the pain she was feeling, and even her mother. I thought it would be terrible if she thought she was going to lose her daughter in an accident like this.

We called our parents and were told to go to Macy's room to wait for them to arrive. We were so scared that maybe Evelyn was dying, and we didn't know what to do. My mom's hug made me feel better for a minute, then it was back to terror. It was the worst feeling ever to know that I might not see Evelyn ever again, or talk to her, or even get a chance to say goodbye to her. I thought that it could have been anyone there that got hurt. Why was it her? I would rather it had been me than her. Why? Why would God do this to her? I guess he does everything for a reason, but why something so terrible?

After the girls were finished trying to explain to us the turn of events, we all walked back inside, and for some reason we gathered again with blank stares around the kitchen island. Maybe a total of only thirty minutes had passed since most of us moms had arrived at the Goodmans' home, but it felt like hours. No one wanted to leave, but there was an awkwardness hanging in the air. None of us knew what we could do to help you at this point, and none of us wanted to look out the window again at that mess of tree in the backyard.

We had contacted many other prayer warriors by this point, so I thought maybe this was our time to pray. I suggested to Maggie and all of the girls there that we pray a Rosary together for you. Everyone seemed delighted to have something to do, and we knew you were in God's hands, so why not put our trust in him for help. We sat in a circle among the chairs and couches in the living room. The pouch of rosaries that I carry in my purse was put to use, and we passed them out for everyone to share.

It was Friday, and the Church recommends praying the Sorrowful Mysteries on Fridays. But with hope in our hearts that we would have something to celebrate, we decided to pray the Joyful Mysteries instead. Leading that Rosary without bawling through the whole thing was so hard for me! Not to mention every time a mom excused herself from the circle to take an urgent phone call we all worried that might be the call bearing bad news. But repeating those Hail Marys, one after the other, and listening to all of your friends' little voices as they recited their prayers was so encouraging and therapeutic for all of us.

When we finished the Rosary, somehow we were all able to take some deep breaths, give some more hugs, and stand up a little straighter.

We pitched in to help Mrs. Goodman prepare some potluck items for a baseball game that night. You were in surgery and we still didn't know the outcome, but the day was moving full steam ahead, and the sun was going to set and rise again and we had to figure out how to deal with it. Finally, we departed on our way to our own homes, where we were forced to deal with our experience of the afternoon on our own.

The timeline of the next forty-eight hours is a bit blurry for me now, but I'm sure your mom has the days detailed down to the minute. There was a flurry of updates via text and email saying that you had survived the surgery on your skull, and the doctors felt optimistic that you would have a good recovery. You survived! We all breathed a little sigh of relief. Somehow, miraculously, the damage was confined to your head and foot (when it seemed like you should have broken bones in your entire body). The surgery on your foot would take place when you got out of the PICU. I found myself asking your mom ridiculous questions via text that later I was worried would come off as insensitive. Questions like, "Will it be months before she's up and walking again?" or "Did they have to shave her head for surgery?" We all had so many questions about your recovery, and it was very difficult to sit back and be patient and let your amazingly strong body and God do the work.

While you were recovering post-surgery in the PICU, mostly only family members visited you at the hospital. Maggie asked relentlessly when she could go and see you. In the meantime, Mr. Legler, the school principal, allowed us to share the news with your entire sixth-grade class, and we offered your classmates the chance to send a card or greeting to the hospital via Mrs. Murphy, who would be visiting you while on "rounds" that Sunday. We were so very touched by the outpouring of support and love from our school to you. Classmates that you weren't particularly close friends with (ie. Kyle, Gabby, Will, Drew) felt the desire to write or send you something to let you know they were sad for you, praying for you, and cared about your recovery. Many teachers and students also reached out to Maggie to see how she was coping, as they all recognized your close friendship and knew she had to be struggling. We felt so blessed by our community.

Maggie was dreading going back to school on Monday without you. Every class was going to be terrible without you there, and she didn't feel up to dealing with all of the questions. She was emotional and tired and wasn't sleeping or resting well, because the visions of that afternoon kept creeping back into her mind when she sat idle or closed her eyes. Unexpectedly, your mom reached out early that Sunday evening stating that you had been released from the PICU, and she asked if Maggie and I would like to visit you that night. This was a gift because Maggie needed to see with her own eyes that you had survived. Maybe if she actually saw that you were going to be okay, then she could go on and go back to school.

We had prepped ourselves that your head would be shaved and that your face would be bruised, and that overall you would look pretty banged up. I was so nervous trying to think of what I'd say to your parents when I saw them. How can you really comfort someone in this situation when you don't fully know the outcome yet? When we arrived and saw you in your hospital room, you looked beautiful! You were resting in bed, and from our angle we couldn't even tell your head was shaved because the surgeon left these long strands of hair near your face, and only one eye was bruised and swollen shut. The biggest difference was that you looked very tiny and frail in that hospital bed, and you had lots of tubes coming out of you assisting with your recovery.

Your mom and dad said that although you were resting, you could still hear what people were saying around you. That night your mom and dad did not stop talking and sharing the details with us of everything that occurred in the past two days. It turns out I didn't need to think of the perfect thing to say, because they didn't need for me to say anything at all. They already knew we were praying for them, and they just needed us to listen. Stories and details were just oozing out of both of them. They wanted to share this story and the emotional roller coaster they'd been on so it was just as real for us as them. I could sense relief in both of them that you'd made it this far, and they felt so optimistic about your recovery.

When it was time for us to go, it seems that your mom wanted you to know for sure that we were there. She leaned down to your left ear *and said in a calm voice, "Evelyn, Maggie is here." Immediately your one, unswollen eye popped open, and you fixed your gaze on Maggie, you managed to slightly smile, and you slowly outstretched your right hand to hers. It looked like it took every ounce of energy in your body to slowly reach out your hand and keep your eye open. You stayed there and held hands for a couple of peaceful minutes. Your mom told you it was okay to rest again, so you sighed and closed your eye, and went back to your restful state again, and we left. Seeing you initially didn't seem so shocking to us, but that moment when you "woke up" and we saw how taxing it was for you to move your little arm was **awful!** We got to the elevator and we both started sobbing. Our car ride home was quiet. When we got home I crawled into Maggie's bed, and I hugged her tight, and we both cried ourselves to sleep. I felt sad for your mom because I knew all she probably wanted to do was hug you tight, but in your fragile state she couldn't do that just yet.*

Over the next couple of days we continued to get updates from your mom that you were making huge strides! Winston was also doing much better at this point. It seemed like all of our prayers were being answered, that you were both going to fully recover. Maggie started writing down all of the little happenings at school to share with you so you wouldn't miss out, and the kids at school started making a video for you to know how much you mean to their class.

I have never seen Maggie so emotional and, at times, so sad. She was scared that when you recovered you may not be the "normal" Evelyn that she knew. She was traumatized by the images and sounds that she witnessed during the accident. She put this in writing:

It's hard to imagine what life would be like without my best friend by my side. She's like a sister to me. This memory will haunt me and stay in my brain forever. This has made a dent in our hearts that will never be filled in the same way. We can never be too grateful for what we have. Always be grateful for what you have, especially your family, friends, and faith.

Maggie was also a little overwhelmed by everyone's desire to be an intimate part of your recovery. The months leading up to the accident she felt so tight in her friendship with you, since at school and on weekends you'd spent every free moment together. Now, with your absence at school, and your time being divided among so many people, Maggie was sad to discover what it felt like to not have you part of her day-to-day life.

On Wednesday of that week we had the opportunity to go and visit you at the hospital again. This time it was arranged that Lauryn Murphy and Maggie would be visiting you at the same time. When we walked into the room it was as if we were visiting a different person. Your mom had washed and styled your hair, you were awake with both eyes open, you were sitting up in bed, and you were using both hands and arms with ease. What a difference a few days made! We literally could not believe it. Your parents offered you girls privacy to visit, so the adults sat outside of your room in the lounge to talk amongst ourselves. Hearing you giggle from inside the room as you chatted with your friends was one of the most joyful sounds I've ever heard. It was affirmation that you were indeed going to be "Evelyn" again. We left that evening smiling instead of crying. Our hope had turned to confidence that everything was going to be okay.

We received the news on Friday morning that you were going to be coming home that afternoon. I gathered with the moms of your friends that were there when the accident happened to decorate your "temporary recovery room" at home. After school that afternoon Lauryn, Maggie, Macy, Lily, Catherine, Anna, and Ava gathered at the Goodmans' home to say a prayer of thanksgiving for your recovery, and for all of the beauty that came out of this terrible tragedy. Then we carpooled to your house to welcome you home. When you walked down the hallway unassisted on your own two feet, and smiled to greet us upon our arrival, it took our breath away. All of that sadness we had felt also seemed to melt away. We all just stood there staring at you in disbelief that this was the same person we saw just days before lying in a hospital bed, so frail, fatigued, and barely conscious. It truly did seem like a miracle.

During the week between the accident and your return home, and the weeks following, people were genuinely enamored with your story. Many of them were total strangers to your family—people who have never even met you. All of the people we shared pieces of your story with, from moms on our boys' "non-Curé" sports teams, to our neighbors and grandparents and extended family members, to the manager at Athleta who graciously replaced your "Friday outfit," have reached out to me many times to find out how you are doing. Everyone always sounds shocked, surprised, and "in awe" of the fact that you are doing so well with really no repercussions.

Even though there are things that may frustrate you right now as you continue to fully recover, to most people you look like a happy, healthy, beautiful, normal seventh grader. I don't know if it is the severity and uniqueness of the accident, your fighting spirit along the way, or your miraculous recovery that draws people to this story. People spend so much time seeing, hearing, witnessing, and experiencing suffering in this world, that maybe it's the "happy ending" that people like the most. One occasional happy ending has the power to refuel people's hope. You endured so much pain through that terrible accident, but through it you have given so many people a great gift. You've given them hope that good things do happen, and that some stories still have happy endings. Thanks for sharing this gift with Maggie and me.

We're so grateful that you are still here to live your life. We're anxious to see what your future has in store for you. Trust in God. He has a plan.

Blessings to You—Maggie and Mrs. Axtell

"Be strong and let your heart take courage, All you who hope in the LORD."
—Psalm 31:24 (NASB)

Chapter 17

Overlease Life

R obbie and I met on the dance floor our junior year at The University of Tulsa, and that was that. He proposed to me when we were twenty-five in Paris at the top of the Eiffel Tower, and I was on top of the world knowing he wanted to spend his whole life with me. As Robbie handed me the pear-shaped diamond engagement ring in the windy heights overlooking Paris, true to his serious, yet funny nature, he cautioned slowly and seriously, "Don't drop this." We married in Springfield, Illinois, on July 1, 2000, at my childhood church, St. Joseph.

Robbie and I share similar backgrounds and are extremely compatible. He tempers my hardheaded feistiness with his even keel. We take good care of one another and love well. We work together. A strong thread of mutual respect and a belief in the importance of loving compromise is woven into our marriage. The man makes me laugh every day, and I count him among the greatest blessings in my life. It is one of my highest aspirations to have a lifelong, happy marriage with this intelligent, hard-working, conscientious, incredible man. We have now been together longer than we lived with our parents.

Our marriage was blessed with four children, and they have provided a never-ending supply of joyful love and crazy stories. I should wear a T-shirt with "Never Dull" on the front because that's how life is with these children in our mix. You can't make up the stuff they say and do.

Family life is fun and maddening, exhilarating and exhausting, rewarding, always interesting, and often a big, loud, hot mess. Add a dog barking at the ruckus, and you get the picture. There are blissful moments when we marvel at the *Leave It to Beaver* or *Little Women* scenes that play out in our household unexpectedly, but they are simply treasured moments—tiny flashes of perfection before one kid says something snarky to another, disputing the color of the sky, and we instantly pop back into real family life again. So it goes. Granted, our life together overflows with abundant love, and the fullness of family joy is the ultimate blessing in this world. I am proud of my vocation as wife and mother, but I admit I get a kick out of introducing myself to new people as an Assets Manager. It's true, and it makes my wise and witty husband smile.

I believe one of our greatest responsibilities as parents is to raise our children with confidence and determination; for some, this looks like a faith component woven into the tapestry of life, to overcome adversity. We want our kids to hear the whisper of "Hope on!" when they need encouragement. I have always been struck by the beauty of the human spirit when faced with something seemingly unsurmountable, like shark-infested waters after a plane crash on a lifeboat with little food for Louis Zamperini in *Unbroken* or St. Maximilian Kolbe's sacrificial acceptance of death by starvation at Auschwitz concentration camp in World War II. Both men had hope. Louis Zamperini believed he could survive. That was his single-minded goal. Kolbe's hope was in Our Father and the promise of salvation and eternal life, so even facing a miserable earthly demise, he was not jaded by the evils around him.

These are extreme examples, but they are powerful, poignant, exemplary models. Life will not be smooth sailing. Are we going to crumple in defeat, or are we going to get back up again after a hard fall? Such attitudes may be taught, and youngsters should be encouraged. Mighty God put a fire in Evelyn. Sometimes, if I'm frank and honest, that makes it challenging to parent her when we have a battle of wills. However, I am thankful for Evelyn's strong streak. I know that personality trait will serve her well over a lifetime.

All we may do is love our children and give parenting our best efforts. Years ago, an assignment came home from school to work as a family to identify key tenets of who we are and the values we represent. We opened that prompt to discussion among our children, took notes, then conferred as parents. Robbie and I aimed to distill the big picture of our goals for raising a great family into a list of ideas we want all our children to feel embedded in their hearts by the time we launch them from our home and into the world. We have a long wooden sign hanging in full sight in our kitchen with these essential reminders.

Know, Love & Serve God

Let Us Remember the Golden Rule

Make Wise Decisions

Love & Support One Another

Speak Kindly

Have an Attitude of Gratitude

Have Patience

Respect Yourself and Others

Tell the Truth

Laugh & Play Hard

Count Your Many Blessings

Believe in Yourself

There Is No Substitute for Hard Work

Pray More

There Is Always HOPE

Give Hugs

Do What Is Right, Not What Is Easy

Say Please and Thank You

Praise God from Whom All Blessings Flow

Stay Strong in Mind and Body

Smile

The Glass Is Half Full

May the Seeds of Faith Flower

In the end we will be judged on how well we loved,

so love with all your heart,

and with all your soul,

and with all your strength.

Heaven Is Our Ultimate Goal

This is a process, and out of the mouths of babes, sometimes our children wisely remind us to follow our own advice. I'll let you speculate on which points they articulate they find us lacking. It may have something to do with patience. Fortunately, we have the blessing of our loving Father in heaven to continuously mold our hearts and form us into the most beautiful versions of ourselves. If we put forth our best effort, and stay the course, there will be unfathomable rewards. That is what happened within my soul the day after Evelyn left the hospital. Out of the blue, my security had been shaken a week prior. Another surprise was ahead: the unexpected pleasure of experiencing the opposite end of the emotional spectrum—elation. It was one fine day for our family!

· · · · · · · · · · · *The Sunday, April 29, 2018 Email Update*
—Alleluia! The BEST Day!

God winks are quite curious, and they abound throughout Evelyn's story. We invited Fr. Storey, our pastor, to have dinner with our family Friday, March 9. He had to cancel due to presiding over a friend's visitation. We attempted to reschedule over spring break in mid-March, but Father was not available until seven weeks later on Friday, April 27. That turned out to be Evelyn's discharge date! When I realized how those events were aligning I decided that we should go forth with our planned dinner in order to break bread together and offer a prayer of thanksgiving for Evelyn's improvement.

We were grateful that my dad and Jane were already staying with us when the accident occurred, and they graciously extended their Kansas City stay to take care of our children. Luckily, I had the blessing of Grandma Jane, who prepared the meal and our home for company after our weeklong stay in the hospital. She's the best. She consistently anticipates needs and meets them without being asked to help. Olivia, Henry, and Vivian were fortunate to be cared for and comforted by such a devoted, kind, and hardworking grandma all week. After reflecting upon that week, my dad wrote, "The hospital activities over seven days generated many strong emotions for many people. The spirit of the Lord, glorious survival, and healing were evident throughout the ordeal. Jane and I tried to keep the home fires burning and the children secure."

At our dinner table Friday night, Fr. Storey reminded me that whatever I wanted to do about rescheduling Vivian's First Communion, he would gladly accommodate. I asked if I was supposed to select a Mass one weekend, and he said he thought we should do something more special than that for Vivian and to celebrate Evelyn's presence with us—her survival. He asked about the next Saturday, May 5. I hesitated, then thought I should simply say what I was wondering without holding back. "I know you have 8 o'clock Mass, two weddings tomorrow (Olivia was altar serving at 10:00 AM for him), and 4 o'clock Mass, and this may be crazy talk, but both sets of grandparents are going back to Illinois and Florida tomorrow. What about doing it tomorrow?" He checked his phone, then said, "How about 9 o'clock tomorrow morning?" I agreed, and with that, he, Robbie, and I started making arrangements and spreading the word for a Saturday, April 28, First Communion. It felt good to be tasked with something like that. I became a woman of action again, in control of one small thing in my out-of-control world.

A close friend quickly reminded me via text that Evelyn's soccer team had a 9:00 AM game. A mother of four with three kids in track, two in soccer, one in baseball, and three taking piano lessons that spring, I find Saturdays are complex logistical beasts for us parents. We are often outnumbered. I thought we'd have to simply go forward with what worked for Father to allow the grandparents to participate in First Communion. Those unable to physically join us for 9:00 AM Mass would surely join us in prayer. (I later learned Evelyn's Curé soccer team joined in pre-game prayer at 9:00 AM, as our Mass began, to dedicate their game to her. Curé won 3-0! I'm sure they missed their spunky midfielder.)

As Father prepared to leave our home, Vivian said, "Can Winston go to church?" "No!" I immediately said. "Dogs don't go to church," Robbie stated the obvious. "Bring him," Fr. Storey casually quipped as he headed out the door with a twinkle in his eyes and a mischievous smile.

The next morning sweet Evelyn bemoaned the fact the we, her seemingly unreasonable parents, would not allow her puppy to attend First Communion even when our priest allowed it. I reached out to Allie, who had developed a bond with Winston after the accident. She had kindly followed up on his care via telephone with the vet and made visits to comfort him while he was away from his family. A plan was made for our dog to go to church. No joke.

Adrienne Doring is a good friend, neighbor, and woman of deep faith. She provided several uplifting, small Scripture signs for us during our hospital stay. I used the blue painter's tape that Katie brilliantly delivered to the hospital to hang cards and signs around the hospital room. I treasured the gentle reminder of faith my heart felt as my eyes fell upon those signs throughout our stay. I shared stories with the medical professionals about the countless prayers coming from Evelyn's accident, and I hope hearts were touched. One young doctor said he would ask his mother to have his hometown parish in western Kansas add Evelyn to a prayer chain. When Adrienne got the text about First Communion she kindly offered to provide photography for us since she had professional equipment from her days before she became a mother. That gift allowed me to be in the moment at Mass, without trying to fumble with my phone to capture the images. I was delighted.

I did not accurately anticipate how much hair had to be done in my house Saturday morning! Evelyn was always self-sufficient with hairstyling endeavors, but she felt naturally self-conscious about the large shaved area on the top of her head. We strategically changed the side of her part and combed her long, beautiful hair over the surgical incision and shaved portion of her head. The result was amazing. People later commented that they couldn't detect anything abnormal about Evelyn's head and hair.

We arrived at church later than planned, and Adrienne swiftly positioned our family on the altar for family photos. I saw people trickle into the church, and the love and concern on their faces was blatantly apparent. We are a community of faith, and there, before us, gathered people who loved us, prayed fervently for us, and were present to celebrate the Eucharist with our family. "Eucharist" means "thanksgiving" or "gratitude." It was perfect. My heart felt so full. Many friends offered their regrets that they were unable to join us due to travel plans, children's sporting events, and conflicts. We understood and expected that, yet we were thrilled by the great turnout with fifteen hours of notice.

The Wednesday prior, April 25, Ashley sent me a video of Vivian singing an *Alleluia* solo and *Taste and See* at the All School Mass. I didn't even realize she was going to sing that day and bawled my eyes out with joy at her sweet, pretty voice, and from sadness that I was forced to miss the live version. I sat on my hospital cot and wept in a moment of pity about the harsh reality of Evelyn's unplanned hospitalization. Ashley tried to cheer me up and put the bug in my ear that once First Communion was rescheduled for Vivian, she should sing her songs again.

Arrangements were made. Christine Brush, a Curé cantor, is a friend of my friend Emily Finlason, and she agreed to sing. Maureen Henderson, not our usual organist, was available to play the piano because our pianist friend and neighbor, Kathy Quigley, already had a commitment. The Mass was absolutely beautiful! I kept looking over my shoulder at the many rows of pews that were filled with supportive friends. We were blessed by the presence of my parents: Dad (Tom) and Jane, Mom (Mary) and Mike. They sat behind us with Jane and Becky, dear friends. Even our puppy, Winston Bear, was with us, sitting with the Goodman family. I think Allie kept our crazy plan from her husband until the last possible second. "Oh, by the way, John, we need to stop at the Overlease's house on our way to church and pick up their dog." Can you imagine the look of shock and dreaded hesitation on his face? He went with it. Winston is a major part of Evelyn's story and brings her immense joy. We are glad for our little pet's continued presence in our lives too.

Vivian's delightful voice rang out with confidence, and my heart swelled with abundant love. Viv has a joy that radiates from her. Darling and charming, she looked stunningly beautiful in her white dress and veil. She handled the postponement of her First Communion with utter grace and maturity quite amazing and beyond what one should expect from an eight-year-old. Evelyn's best friend's twin brother, Grant Axtell, was the altar server, which pleased me immensely. My father was lector for the first reading with his sure, deep voice. Dad has always been a solid, reassuring, loving part of my life. Time and again during the Mass the special details of loved ones' participation caused peace and happiness to wash over me. I experienced unbridled joy. My cup overflowed. There was a song in my heart that morning. God was with us.

The gospel was from John 14:7–14 with the tremendous encouragement, "Whatever you ask in my name, I will do." Fr. Storey gave a great homily reminding us, "Ask and you shall receive." We did. God answered our prayers. After Father spoke of Jesus' sacrifice on the cross for us, Evelyn leaned over and whispered with her usual wit and a smidge of sarcasm, "Jesus took the cross. I took the tree." Everything about the ceremony was happy, uplifting, joyful. I selected *You Are Mine* by David Haas, and as always, it moved me to tears. Those lyrics. Wow, how I could relate to them.

> *I will come to you in the silence,*
> *I will lift you from all your fear.*
> *You will hear My voice,*
> *I claim you as My choice,*
> *Be still and know I am here.*
>
> *I am hope for all who are hopeless,*
> *I am eyes for all who long to see.*
> *In the shadows of the night,*
> *I will be your Light,*
> *Come and rest in Me.*
>
> Refrain
>
> *Do not be afraid, I am with you.*
> *I have called you each by name.*
> *Come and follow Me,*
> *I will bring you home;*
> *I love you and you are Mine.*

I am strength for all the despairing,
Healing for the ones who dwell in shame.
All the blind will see, the lame will all run free,
And all will know My Name.

Refrain

I am the Word that leads all to freedom.
I am the Peace the world cannot give.
I will call your name, embracing all your pain,
Stand up, now walk, and live!

Refrain

It was the best Mass I have ever attended, and I couldn't help reflecting on the blessing that many of those who love us were gathered in joyful, heartfelt thanks and celebration for Vivian's sacrament and Evelyn's survival, not supporting us as we mourned an immeasurable loss at a funeral for our young daughter. The latter could have been our fate. Not this time. God has plans for Evelyn. Again and again, we learned of groups of people who were made aware of the accident and stormed heaven with prayers for her survival and recovery. There is power in prayer. I believe in him. Today at Sunday Mass a mother touched my shoulder and quietly and tenderly said, "I'm so happy for your miracle." I wonder if my tears will ever run dry.

Ave Maria, Robbie's favorite hymn, was sung beautifully by Christine when Vivian proceeded to the altar to receive her First Communion. It was a moment I had eagerly anticipated Vivian's entire second grade year. I was thrilled for my youngest, and I had the perfect front-row view of the moment. I couldn't contain my emotions any longer. I cried hard and attempted to hold back loud sobs as Vivian was offered the Bread of Life, Jesus. Henry told me, "Mom, you are going to flood the church!" It was all too much to keep inside. I was so deeply, incredibly, beyond what words may ever adequately express, grateful, exuberant, and joyful. When our puppy, Winston, was led on a leash up to the altar during the communion line by Macy, my tears turned to free-flowing, hearty laughter. YOU CAN'T MAKE UP THIS STUFF!

As Mass ended, Father invited Vivian and our immediate family to walk out with him in a recessional, and we were able to look with gratitude into the faces of those gathered to celebrate with us. All of the smiles blessed our hearts. Many eyes were wet. Tight, long hugs that friends had waited days to offer communicated through human touch what words can't convey, and I couldn't stop sobbing.

The sun shone upon us. In the words of my beloved father, "It was a GLORIOUS day!" My puppy frolicked around with always-active Henry. Vivian happily received sweet words of congratulations. Evelyn looked remarkably well, even though her foot hurt a lot by that point. We had lived through the most traumatic, mentally draining and physically exhausting week of our lives, and we not only survived, but we also had a tremendous, magnificent, splendid, perfect, happy ending. We celebrated the gift of the Eucharist surrounded by the love of family and friends, which provided peace, hope, and the ultimate demonstration of living faith. Praise be to God.

"This is the day the LORD *has made; let us rejoice and be glad in it."*
—Psalm 118:24

"May the God of hope fill you with all joy and peace as you trust in him, so that you may overflow with hope by the power of the Holy Spirit."
—Romans 15:13 (NIV)

Chapter 18

What a Difference a Week Makes

· · · · · · · · · *Friday, May 4, 2018—1:45 PM Email Update*

A s I begin this summary of Evelyn's first week out of the hospital after
the accident, we are approaching, nearly to the hour, the two-week
mark since she was injured. Evelyn came home from CMH at this time of
day one week ago last Friday after seven nights. I am so happy right now.
Her week has gotten progressively better, day by day. I trust that's how her
recovery will progress, slow and steady.

We moved Evelyn into the guest bedroom on the first floor to keep her
close to our bedroom and prevent her from navigating the stairs with an
injured, bulkily bandaged foot. The seven girls present at the Goodmans'
house the day of the accident and their moms surprised Evelyn with a bit
of a guest-room makeover when she got home. They added some pops
of teal blue that Evelyn loves. On a bulletin board, photos of Evelyn and
friends were displayed with a sweet sign from the girls, "You are strong,
brave, and beautiful." They strung cord from corner to corner with mini
clothespins to hang Evelyn's cards. Tears spilled over as I read a sign,
"Faith can move mountains," stunned by our friends' efforts. Evelyn
turned around slowly to take it all in, marveling at the amazing transfor-
mation; she "oohed and aahed." Katie had said the girls wanted to do a
little something to decorate the room before Evelyn's arrival—simple and
tasteful. I envisioned butcher paper with kids' messages in marker! Our
friends shocked us! We felt truly loved and were simply delighted by the
sweet gesture.

Winston's exuberant tail wagging demonstrated his absolute delight at Evelyn's return home. As a result of his head injury, he held his head tilted sideways, which always looked cute. Our puppy still had neurological deficits and tipped over backward in slow motion when he reared up to greet us. Likewise, when he hiked his leg to pee, he slowly tipped over sideways. Often, he startles easily, flailing his limbs out of control, skidding and slipping on our hardwood floors like Bambi on a frozen pond. It looked comical, but it was a sad example of the extent of his brain trauma. We hoped Winston's balance and agility would return. Henry and Vivian's rambunctious play sometimes overwhelmed our poodle, and our dog let the kids know that he wanted to be left alone by nipping. His manner was milder following the accident; his docile nature caused Henry to exclaim, "The accident made Winston nicer!"

I put a little silver bell on Evelyn's nightstand, since I wanted to make sure she could get my attention even with her weak voice. The first morning that she woke up at home, she coughed at 6:10 AM. She didn't need her bell, because I raced to her bedside. I slept lightly on high alert all night, just like a mother with a newborn baby. Her words made my heart sing, they were so sweet. "You came to my rescue. You love me! I wondered if you'd come."

Evelyn was in great pain Sunday at church, less than forty-eight hours after hospital discharge. Robbie immediately slipped out with her as Mass ended; she had reached the limit of her stamina for the outing. I stayed and received hugs from several friends. Their sympathetic eyes and embraces spoke volumes—no words were necessary.

The first days at home were challenging—dramatically up and down. Sometimes we felt forced to pull the reins to hold Evelyn back from doing too much, then at other times she'd crash in pain and exhaustion, sleeping for long stretches during the daytime. For instance, I was shocked on Sunday when I heard Evelyn call out, "Hey, Mom, where is my tennis shoe?!" She only needed one since her wounded foot was wrapped in a bandage and she wore a type of protective boot. Evelyn and Olivia volleyed tennis balls in our uneven driveway. Evelyn hobbled around with only one sturdy foot, and I couldn't believe my eyes. Moments like that struck me with tremendous fear for her safety. Her head had just been sawed open and put back together. Her brain was bruised and inflamed. In truth, I wanted to wrap my child in bubble wrap and keep her inside on a comfy piece of furniture. Fear that she would come to further harm consumed my thoughts. Parenting with a trusting heart is extremely difficult after a traumatic event.

Within a few days she finished the prescriptions (antibiotics and other medication) sent home with us, and she has refused all other over-the-counter (or stronger) pain medicine available to her. She doesn't like taking medicine, and she insisted she didn't need it. So be it. My girl is strong, and I respect her fire and mental toughness.

She had three medical follow-up appointments this week. She was cleared by Occupational Therapy. We were told the best therapy is for her to do the stuff she likes to do—just play. The stitches were removed from her foot on Wednesday by the plastic surgeon, and she is much more comfortable with her new, cushioned bandage, and sleeker foot wrap. She can wear a tennis shoe—major progress. The top of her foot is still battered and bruised, but Dr. Kaye expects it to heal in two more weeks. She has a tender, superficial area of skin that is raw and abraded, but her skin is trying to grow back. She now has a large, curved, discolored scar that resembles a big bite mark. Robbie told her that one day when she's a momma she'll be able to tell her child she was bitten by a shark! He proudly tells our children tales of battles he has had with wild beasts that resulted in a scar on his forehead.

Evelyn's close friends have visited, and their laughter has truly been the best medicine for all of us. I have accepted needed childcare help from our neighbor, Sue May, our piano teacher, Ms. Amy Gardner, and my book club OB/GYN friend, Cori Cooper—as we may not leave Evelyn home alone yet post-operation. Vivian was ill and I had to take her to the pediatrician's office. Cori generously gave of her time on her day off work to come to my aid. Evelyn told Dr. Cooper with a not-so-pleased, rather smug voice, "I used to babysit; now I get babysat." We have been blessed with some cuddle time from the Nicksons' little John Paul and the Schlicks' sweet Selma, which is perfect for baby lovers like Evelyn and me!

Mrs. Pickett, Evelyn's favorite elementary school teacher, came over one afternoon. Our accomplished and lovely pediatrician, Natasha Burgert, MD, made a house call to spend time visiting with Evelyn and save us the effort of yet another trip to a medical appointment. She brought the gift of her family's favorite games—pretty amazing. We are most grateful for the love and care.

Evelyn loves being outside with her puppy. We often sit on our patio, bask in the warm sun, hang out, and chat. Today, I had the courage to write about the afternoon of the accident, and I wept at my laptop as Evelyn relaxed in a chair with Winston. I warned her ahead of time that what I planned to write was going to be emotionally difficult for me. On Wednesday, Robbie had the afternoon off from his usual surgery schedule, so he invited us to go out for lunch if Evelyn felt up to it. The outing was a celebration of life.

Evelyn looks pretty fantastic. She walks with only a slight limp. She and I did a no-impact workout this morning in which yoga poses were held for forty-five seconds. Balance and strength were required, and she worked hard with just some slight foot pain and position modifications. I was quite proud of her. I haven't done anything for fitness for two weeks either, so it felt good to ease into a workout with my sweet girl. Her hair is growing back on her scalp where it was shaved, and with proper styling the buzzed area is not very evident. Robbie and I think she looks gorgeous.

The highlight of the week came this afternoon when she visited school for an outdoor pizza party hosted by Pie Five Pizza Co. and Fr. Storey. Evelyn was welcomed on a sunshiny day with a sign and a large group of excited classmates who ran to greet her. She was so happy to see everyone, and she even managed to eat a slice of pizza with her fractured mandible. Ev felt well enough that she asked to stay for recess after lunchtime ended. She walked around the playground with her friends, and I think she felt like a normal sixth-grade girl for a bit.

Upon returning home, we received an email from her classroom teacher, Mr. Greer, in which the kids made a wacky and wonderful Get Well Video. It was fun to listen to Evelyn belly laugh with gusto. The kid actors were cute, some downright hilarious with their deadpan countenances, and we both appreciated the kind and creative gift. The students achieved their goal to lift Evelyn's spirits and brighten her day.

Evelyn's Great-Uncle John sent her a fitting and humorous "Kick-Ass Mode Activated" card, which made her eyebrows go up, with a blue dog collar and leash. From classmate Chris Barreca's family she received a Willow Tree Angel of Friendship Animal Lover figurine of a girl holding a puppy in her loving arms, and that started my tears flowing. It was perfect. Evelyn LOVED the gifts.

She is making progress. Yesterday, Evelyn woke up, and her eye was not black, purple, or dark pink! It looked nearly normal. Her headaches appear to be fading. She is gaining range of motion and strength in her injured foot. This morning when I placed breakfast before her, she simply ate it—all of it! We will continue providing opportunities for Evelyn's body and brain to recuperate, and we believe she will heal and recover in time.

The timing of the accident, just a few weeks before school ends for summer break, is a blessing too. I am not worried about her "getting well soon to hurry back to school." I know she has worked as a diligent student all year, and the administration and teachers have been totally supportive about the importance of allowing her time to stay home, rest, and heal.

Thank you for your continued prayers of thanksgiving for Evelyn's speedy advancements and for prayers for future healing. Evelyn is our little dynamo, and she won't be held back for long. Likewise, it has been such a gift to know we have the support of our family, friends, our faith-filled school, church, and neighborhood community to support us with transportation to the kids' sports events, childcare when I must leave home, gift cards to restaurants, and home-cooked meals. We feel absolutely loved, wrapped in helpful arms, and we greatly value the blessing you all are to our family. We promise to help you in your times of need as life deals out difficult hands.

Two weeks ago right now, my family's life changed with the crack of a tree limb. Life was not ended. For that we are eternally grateful. We rejoice! A small body was injured. Life was not ruined. Parental security was shattered like smashed glass, our hearts left exposed to the shards. Damaged. Broken. Powerless.

By the power and grace of God we have a happy ending for our child. We believe God will provide what we need no matter the circumstances, and we believe the doctors' positive prognosis for Evelyn and trust in complete healing for her in the months ahead. We will keep praying. *"If you remain in me and my words remain in you, ask for whatever you want and it will be done for you. By this is my Father glorified, that you bear much fruit and become my disciples."*—John 15:7–8

A friend expressed the heartfelt willingness of those dear to us— our tribe, as she called our people—to be the hands and feet of Jesus on earth to serve our family and carry us through the initial crisis and beyond. She saw this vital endeavor as the Body of Christ working together to restore Evelyn, which is a stunningly beautiful image of God's love manifested in our world. She wrote, "She's not just your daughter, but belongs to all of us. We are Team Evelyn! Love you, Love her, Love Jesus!" Many people lived my friend's message, and we humbly thank each one. Our tribe carried us. We felt the love. We return the love.

The Portuguese proverb "God writes straight with crooked lines" speaks volumes when we contemplate how it applies to our lives. Ultimately, he will get us to a place where Evelyn's body is completely healed and this mother's emotions from living through a traumatic event will level out once more. We don't have access to the architect's master plan or know the last line of the book. We are simply on the journey of life, and we may get rerouted from our intended path from time to time. Every reader has experienced this reality.

One of the women in my Scripture study expressed, "God's plan for us takes many turns in life. It moves forward despite all the messiness. The plan is not always obvious to us, but we must trust and have faith." Terry Gillcrist, a cancer survivor in our group, said, "Sometimes something comes out of nowhere and our world is rocked, but God is our rock." These notions are true of our faith walk over the course of a lifetime too. "In the terrain of spiritual life, we need guides," wrote Henri Nouwen. These guides may come in the form of friends, religious leaders, or experiences that influence us along our way.

God answered our prayers to save Evelyn's life. Pure and beautiful and awe-inspiring and simple—she lived! She is her sweet self. She will be fully physically restored in God's time. Were there protective angels around her? Yes. I choose to believe—yes.

He has used her accident and the love and faith of our community to demonstrate his goodness. Sometimes life shakes us up. Sometimes an event forces everything that was in motion in our life to come to a screeching halt—even though we desperately, to the depths of our being, wish to maintain the status quo of our previous, easier, steady course! We must bear in mind there exists the promise that God is with us. Always. No matter what. God told Isaac in Genesis 26:24, "*You have no need to fear, since I am with you.*"

Deacon Steve White's homily on the virtue of trust is relevant since oppressive fear sometimes torments souls.

"Do I really trust that God loves me so much that He will always take care of me? God is a loving and caring Father. In His great goodness He is deeply concerned about every little aspect of our lives, He really is. Jesus tells us over and over again in the Gospels how much the Father cares about His beloved sons and daughters—you and me. Jesus wants to see us filled with His serenity and peace—at all times and in all circumstances.

"I think we can say we believe that—in our minds. But deep down in our hearts do we really believe that—to the point where it influences how we live our lives? When the tribulations and misfortunes of life hit us, worry overwhelms us. In the face of great trials—fear grips us. We get into difficult situations in life. All our efforts to fix it or work our way out achieve nothing and we get discouraged. We lose hope.

"Imagine how much worry, fear, and anxiety we could save ourselves if we could really trust in the goodness of God and abandon ourselves to His loving care. I don't mean abandon ourselves in some foolish way and just sit back and do nothing. But to say, 'Lord, I'm not sure why I'm in this situation, but I know in Your providential goodness You have allowed it to happen. I choose to entrust myself and this situation to You. Jesus, I trust in You. Show me the next step and give me the

strength to take it.' When we have complete trust in God, using whatever normal human means are necessary in each situation, Our Lord gives us incomparable serenity and strength."

It is a true spiritual gift that I may sit in my church and listen to such an inspiring, soul-fueling message. Let true trust in God be our goal in this uncertain world. We should all strive to be like Abraham of the Old Testament, ready to trust with an open heart and the message, "Here I am, Lord." He was the epitome of one who accepted a plan from God that no human could understand. Life is a mystery. Faith will help us unravel it and find meaning in our trials. For there will be trials.

Have faith. Hope on! God is good.

Closed at 2:44 PM (The 911 call at the accident was placed at 2:46 PM).

Chapter 19

Revisiting the Yard—My Epiphany

I turned forty-four on May 20. With so many people from my generation struggling with life-threatening health challenges, I'm deeply grateful for each healthy year I may share with the ones I love. However, like most, I feel like my age should be a smaller number.

The second school day that Evelyn was home from the hospital, our second grader, Vivian, stayed home sick with allergy-related breathing issues. As she rested she used my laptop to search out inspirational sayings. Olivia once made a sign that read, "No beauty shines brighter than that of a good heart." We saw that phrase in Magical Scraps, a boutique, on a trip in Breckenridge, Colorado, and Olivia painted it for me on a canvas that is displayed in our master bathroom. Little Vivian reads it daily as I braid or style her long hair. It is her favorite. She decided to find more uplifting quotes to cheer us all. This gesture demonstrates her sweet heart and caring nature. Vivian wrote each find in pencil on a piece of notebook paper in her childlike penmanship to make a cute book, which gave Olivia the idea to turn them into a "real" book for my birthday gift.

The cover says, "Life is tough, but so are you.—A Book of Inspiration." During family dinner, provided by yet another dear friend, Robbie shared his favorite saying from the book, "Only in darkness can you see the stars," by Martin Luther King Jr. He told us that to him that phrase sums up our experience over the last several weeks. Robbie read the *Harry Potter* series with Olivia when she was younger, so she included a wise Dumbledore quote in my collection, "Happiness can be found even in the darkest of times if one only remembers to turn on the light." To me, light always represents the light of Christ, all that is good and pure, hope when faced with adversity.

We had a mountain to climb starting April 20, 2018, but we were not forced to go it alone. Our whole family recognizes the truth that we were lifted by the love and prayers of family, friends, school and church members, neighbors (some of whom we had never yet met); strangers who learned of Evelyn's accident through their friends, coworkers, or family; and various groups of people we have connected with far back in the past and recently: college friends, past and current coworkers, and our new Notre Dame de Sion community. It was humbling and utterly amazing.

I share this as I reflect upon the darkness that still sometimes grips me as though I'm held in the clutches of a monster's fist when memories of the accident strike. Rushing to Evelyn, discovering her, still and seemingly dead, then witnessing the magnitude of her pain, hearing her wailing, fearing she was made blind and deaf from serious head injuries, put my heart and mind in a place of complete despair. Those minutes in the grass, holding my bleeding, out-of-her-mind-from-pain child in my arms as I implored her to fight and stay awake, were a rock-bottom low. In that time of alarm, the scale was tipped precariously toward losing Evelyn forever.

"Hail Mary, full of grace, the Lord is with thee. . . ." That's all I could get out, over and over. "Evelyn, Jesus loves you! I love you!!" It moves me to tears just writing the words I repeated like a broken record. In the end, two things matter most: love and God.

Our time in the yard, immediately following the accident, clenched my heart. All my children, each for their own personal reasons, wanted to go back to the yard to see "The Tree." I think Olivia felt anger and wanted in some way to pay back the tree for the pain and suffering it caused her innocent little sister and family. I think Henry and Vivian needed a visual to make sense of an accident that resulted in such serious injury to their big sister that their mother never returned home from the hospital to care for them for over a week. Evelyn didn't even remember Macy's backyard or the accident, so she wanted to go back to piece together the clips she heard in the hospital from family and school friends who were in the backyard when the tree limb cracked and fell.

I really didn't want to go back. Ever. My memories were too vivid. The cut to my heart was too deep. The horror was still so real when I replayed the scene that it created strong negative physical responses within me. However, as I think about my inner discourse, I knew deeply the wisdom of Olivia's book cover before it was ever given to me, "Life is tough, but so am I!" I could go back to the accident scene for my children.

We returned exactly two weeks after the accident. The day was distinctly beautiful, bright, and mild, and a gentle breeze moved the air. Robbie parked our minivan on the street in front of the Goodmans' driveway. We all climbed out, and as I began walking toward the driveway and my eyes fell on the fence, I unexpectedly—as I had been totally fine up to that moment—burst into sobs. It was heartrending to see the privacy fence. With one glance, it was April 20 again.

Upon first hearing the crack of the tree limb as it broke free of the trunk, my eyes shot upward. However, the fence image is indelibly imprinted in my brain. There was a rush of frantic movement on the other side of the fence as the huge limb came crashing down. The point in time when the girls ran for safety marked the point where it was still possible that everything was all right in my world . . . until I reached the fence.

I will never forget the moment when my running brought me to the fence. I saw my daughter though the gap in the wooden slats. It was instantly apparent that everything was far from fine, and the fence stood as a physical blockade that prevented me from rushing to Evelyn's aid. The fence image is powerful and painful in my mind. It is also full of symbolism.

It took me a little while to calm down on the evening that we returned to the yard. Robbie provided the comfort that comes from his physical presence, his warm embrace and strong hand enclosing mine, along with his calm demeanor. The kids were unaffected. They raced ahead of me and shot into the backyard as though entering a park where they intended to play. Bless them. I felt much more tentative about entering the yard, like walking on a rickety pedestrian rope bridge over a deep ravine. Shaky. Uncertain. Taking each step with trepidation.

Once inside the backyard, I struggled to make sense of the lay of the land. The location of the tree in relation to the perimeter fences was not in line with my mind's eye memory. I gazed upon the tree. Although the major limb that lay on the ground near the trunk was significant in diameter and could easily have been deadly after falling from such a height, it was not a stately, massive oak. It was a willow tree. There were several other long segments of branches that had been moved out of the way and dragged over to the fence line for mowing to occur. I tried to put the X's on my mental map of the backyard, and everything just seemed off from what I remembered. It was unsettling, and I felt very confused and troubled.

I gathered our family under the tree near the large, fallen hunk of limb. We held hands in a circle and prayed together. My voice faltered. Tears filled my eyes, escaped, and I struggled to speak. I wanted to offer praise to God for the blessing of Evelyn's surviving the accident, but it touched my inner core to stand in that physical location with our intact family of six. Likewise, I was struck by Evelyn's slight frame as she stood near the long, heavy tree limb on the ground. The Holy Spirit allowed me to utter a prayer of thankfulness for God's love and goodness.

Allie gave us access to enter her property and a promise of privacy. However, she told me in advance that she would sit on her front porch during our visit should we need anything. I went to her in tears and asked for her help to show me where Evelyn lay fallen in the backyard.

We walked to a bare spot on the ground where the impact of the limb had stripped the grass from the earth with the force of its impact. She said there was blood near that spot that the rain had since washed away.

Again, I cried. I cried hard. I hung my head and wept. A mother broken and bereft. I felt so tired and beaten down, emotionally weak. Allie put her arm around my shoulders and comforted me without words. I turned in a circle and took it all in for a few moments. What made the biggest impression on me was the short distance between where Evelyn fell to the ground and the spot where the big, heavy limb landed. A few mere feet, and her back would have been broken by the blow. There were angels among us that afternoon. I believe it.

The memory of the yard hurts. Dag Hammarskjöld of the United Nations spoke words that remind us to trust God's plan. "For all that has been, thanks. For all that will be, yes." Evelyn suffered. Her suffering was short-lived in comparison to that of children who fight for their lives during lengthy cancer battles, but her unusual accident and the aftermath were a cross to bear for our family nonetheless. We have to take it all, and accept every bit—the good, the ugly, the bad. All of it molds us. Each experience makes us who we are. Every challenge is an opportunity to grow, to overcome, to persevere through adversity with trust in God's plan.

A truly heroic Catholic man, Dr. Takashi Nagai, while dying from leukemia from effects of radiation exposure, said in *A Song for Nagasaki: The Story of Takashi Nagai: Scientist, Convert, and Survivor of the Atomic Bomb*, "Suffering, gratefully accepted, refines the human heart, and the experience of darkness sharpens the vision of the spirit."

I often remind my children that it is important to maintain proper perspective. Even when we face significant challenges, it is not uncommon to find others enduring even greater difficulties. It could always be worse. We may spend a day in the sunshine and totally take the sunlight for granted, only longing for it after a stretch of gloomy, rainy, dismal days. Recall the physical sensation of traveling through a dark tunnel on a little train at the zoo, or through a stretch of pitch black on a roller coaster, or on an interstate through a mountain tunnel. Sometimes that darkness threatens our sense of security and makes us feel uneasy. Like an insecure child alone in a pitch-black bedroom, we don't always like the dark. Once we exit the tunnel and emerge into the light of day again, we are struck by the vivid contrast between the dark and the light. We enjoy a moment of deep appreciation for the light and the security it brings to us. The same happens when we survive the darkness of hard times, only it happens to our souls. This is life-changing. Suffering embraced can have a beautiful impact on our interior life. In the acceptance of our lot in life we may turn our innermost dial to "thankful for everything, all the time."

After I calmed down, and the children—shockingly, even hobbling Evelyn—left the yard to shoot baskets in the driveway, I looked up and noticed hanging strands of small, delicate willow leaves slightly swaying in the breeze. Voices of children rang out in the neighborhood and birds chirped. There was beauty in the tree, even after everything that happened to my girl as a result of the tree's failure to remain strong and upright. God was there in that moment for my peace, and I will never forget the gift of that moment of clarity.

The next morning, a Saturday, while enjoying a rare weekend opportunity to relax in bed with a cup of hot coffee next to Robbie, I decided to read *Searching for and Maintaining Peace—A Small Treatise on Peace of Heart* by Fr. Jacques Philippe, which was a gift from Adrienne while I was in the hospital with Evelyn.

Unbelievable to me, I read the following: "God is a God of peace. He does not speak and does not operate except in peace, not in trouble and agitation. Let us remember the experience of the prophet Elijah of Horeb: God was not in the hurricane, nor the earthquake, nor in the fire, but in the *whisper of a gentle breeze.*" —1 Kings 19!

I turned to Robbie and excitedly told him about my final moments in the yard the previous evening after he left with the children. I described the epiphany of that moment as I marveled at God's creation while the Holy Spirit's peace and grace washed over me. I will describe it again. Picture it! Put yourself in my shoes in that infamous yard. Rays of sunlight filtered through the trees casting scattered shadows; exquisite, faint music of birds colored the air; little children squealed with delight; the wind took the tree that nearly killed my little girl and ever so gently rustled the long, slender, willowy wisps of leaves. It was quite breathtaking, and through God's grace that peaceful moment is also indelibly imprinted in my soul. Thanks be to God! His grace is enough for us.

When I left the place where Evelyn's accident occurred, I felt as though most of the power that the memories of "the yard" had over me had been diminished. The monster had released his death grip, and I was free once more. Returning to the accident site was difficult, but it was the right thing to do. After that visit, I felt empowered with control of my memories.

Vivid flashbacks may hit me for decades to come, bringing forth a flood of emotion and anxiety, but that's all right. The accident is a part of my life, and I can handle the memories. I marvel at the juxtaposition of accepting my brokenness and yet feeling inner strength. I believe that if we prayerfully strive for a grateful heart by intentionally and frequently offering prayers of thanks for God's abundant blessings—the tiny delights of daily life and even the life-changing, difficult ones—we will live in deliberate, faithful trust and may walk a road, however circuitous, that leads to interior peace.

Obviously, this is the process of a lifetime. We are all on a spiritual journey. We take baby steps toward growing the seeds of our faith more often than making leaps and bounds. As every adult knows, the roads we encounter in life are winding, with hills and valleys, and a few dead ends, and they are sometimes terribly rocky—utter mountains. God never promised his people a life devoid of suffering. The good thing about our journey is that we only take one step at a time, and God is with us each step of the way.

"By waiting and by calm you shall be saved, in quiet and in trust your strength lies." —Isaiah 30:15

Chapter 20:
Abundant Hope

· · · · · · · · · · · · · *Thursday, May 10, 2018 Email Update*
(Nearly three weeks after the accident and after two weeks spent
recovering at home)

W e've all heard about "waiting to exhale" or a "sigh of relief." At Evelyn's post-op neurosurgery appointment, Dr. Kaufman took one look at her and said, "She'll have a complete recovery with no long-term problems." I felt like kissing him (on the cheek!) and jumping up and down! Evelyn reported, "My head doesn't hurt." We asked a slew of questions about Evelyn's resuming physical activities, and Dr. Kaufman told us she must hold back for a time, but she was moving in the right direction.

Evelyn's doctor made us laugh when I told him about us worrying about her playing laser tag with siblings on the driveway. He explained that her skull is protected in its current state (a few titanium plates) from most things, barring unforeseen trauma. He went on to explain that if she falls, she will most likely hit her forehead or the back of her head, the thicker parts of the human skull. A blow to the top of the head, where she was injured and had surgery, in the normal course of activities, would be a low risk. He went on, "If she's hanging upside down or something falls out of the sky . . ." Evelyn and I looked at each other, burst out laughing, and I said, "Like a large tree limb?!" He stated the obvious, that such an accident would be extremely rare. Dr. Kaufman is a steady man.

She's going to experience peaks and valleys in her days on the road to complete healing, but just as my sensible husband previously stated, the highs and lows will become closer together. She'll have a CT in a year to make sure the bone healing has sealed appropriately. Immediately following Evelyn's emergency neurosurgery, her doctor apologized profusely about the "bad haircut" he gave her. At the time, we were so overwhelmingly thankful for the good surgical outcome that we dismissed his words and thanked Dr. Kaufman for saving Evelyn's life. "We're just glad her brain is okay!" I said. Today, I told him that her chief complaint through this experience has been her shaved head. He got it. In his fourteen years in this field, he said that his patients with brain tumors who required surgery did not inquire about their brain tumors. They inquired about their hair growth. Hair matters to adolescents and teenagers. Evelyn's hair is growing back quickly, and her oddly shaped head scar is on her scalp, hidden by hair, not across her pretty face. Time will heal this wound, and her hair will disguise it for a lifetime.

One major point of frustration for Evelyn is that after being a babysitter and experiencing the independence of being mature enough to be left home alone, post-surgery, she requires someone to stay with her when her parents must leave home. She is almost to the end of this annoyance, as she sees the situation. I was told that the future duration depends upon my comfort level. She said to me in private, "That means I can be left alone—as long as you're not a chicken." That's my spunky Ev. She knows me. She doesn't sugarcoat her comments. I am a chicken. I understand that about myself. I expect this too shall pass.

What she doesn't understand is that I am still afraid she will have a seizure from her brain injury, and I certainly don't want her to experience such an episode while she is home alone or with siblings. The probability of such an occurrence is low, yet I suspect the incidence of tree limbs falling and hitting someone on the head is rather low too. Sometimes bad things happen. I worry about all my family members falling victim to some terrible fate. I'm stuck in a rut of worry, and it is challenging to accept that I will soon need to allow Evelyn to spread her wings and assert some independence. My instinct tells me to put her under my protective wing and keep her there indefinitely, safe from harm.

She's so tough that she doesn't complain about pain or limp from her injured foot, nor does her wound slow her down. We have spied her running slightly. Robbie said, "If we can't slow her down, we may need to make her wear a helmet." He was serious. Luckily for Evelyn, her doctors are thrilled that she is getting back to her active lifestyle one day at a time. They want her to eat a lot, rest a lot, and do things she enjoys while her brain continues to heal. She is currently undertaking a project designing and creating a 3D home model out of recycled material, which is back in line with her creative endeavors.

I have been a stay-at-home mom since Olivia, our first child, was born in 2003. This has been one of the greatest blessings that Robbie and I have known for our own family. I mourned the start of school for each of my children. I hung on tightly to Vivian. Out of seventy-five full-day kinder-garten students, she was one of only two students whose parents opted for half-day attendance. A lovely friend texted me, "I hope your time at home with Evelyn is blessed with continued healing, special bonding, and moments of quiet peace…and good calorie consumption. Stay strong, sister!" Nikki nailed it! I cherished the days when my kids were home with me, and Evelyn and I are absolutely enjoying this amazing time together. This is one good that will come of her suffering. We are together.

Evelyn went to school for a short time on Tuesday, and she will return this afternoon to watch project presentations. I know Evelyn feels as if she's living the dream by being able to cherry-pick which end-of-school-year activities she attends. We are thankful to the teachers for welcoming her participation as she is able.

I went for a run through our neighborhood in the six o'clock hour this morning, and it felt wonderful. I have an appetite again, and I'm resting fairly well. Life is good. Robbie and I marvel at Evelyn. She looks so good that it is almost incomprehensible to recall those early moments when the scale was tipped so precariously toward the worst. Evelyn is thriving. She received a pretty journal, and on it is the quote, "And though she be but little, she is fierce." It makes me smile. It makes me cry. We are happy for each day, icing on the beautiful cake that is our daughter, and we have hope in a bright tomorrow for Evelyn.

A prayer sent by Katie's parents, Don and Shirley Fasbender, provides comfort: "Your hope, dear God, transforms every aspect of my life: anxiety and fear are diminished in the light of hope; doubt becomes confidence with the grace of hope." Those words resonate with us—beautiful and true. We must aspire to live by their promise.

Last night Vivian asked me to read with her from her new Bible, and God gave us a wink. I told her I always like Romans, and I randomly opened to this in chapter five:

> Faith, Hope and Love. —Therefore, since we have been justified by faith, we have peace with God through our Lord Jesus Christ, through whom we have gained access (by faith) to this grace in which we stand, and we boast in hope of the glory of God. Not only that, but we even boast of our afflictions, knowing that afflictions produce endurance, and endurance, proven character, and proven character, hope, and hope does not disappoint, because the love of God has been poured out into our hearts through the Holy Spirit that has been given to us.

I prayed with Vivian, tucked her in with a kiss goodnight, and rushed to Evelyn's room to share my discovery with her. I've always loved that verse, but the message has never meant more to me than when applied to the meaning that I now see in the suffering my little girl endured. The experience of the accident will help form Evelyn's character, faith, and heart. We are left with the wonderful gifts of abundant hope, trust in God's plan, and loving, grateful hearts. In such light, her accident was a blessing.

"I know that you can do all things, and that no purpose of yours can be hindered. I have dealt with great things that I do not understand; things too wonderful for me, which I cannot know." —Job 42:2–3

Chapter 21:
Letting Go

When Evelyn went to school I was nervous about her getting accidentally pummeled by rambunctious middle-school boys in the gym where walkers gather at the end of the day. I had to pray for trust and remember the neurosurgeon's words about the current strength of her skull.

I walked with Winston toward Mission Road to meet Evelyn, Henry, and Vivian on their way home from school for the first time in over three weeks. It was surreal. Vivian ran to me first, thrilled that I was finally walking to meet her again. Next, Evelyn appeared happily holding a blue helium balloon. In order to create no doubt in my mind about God's sense of humor, Henry sprinted toward me, talking nonstop about the baby chipmunk he just found, which he immediately insisted we keep as a pet. I explained to Henry that he had taken a nursing baby mammal away from its mother. He had to put it back. He didn't want to put it back. "He's clinging to me, Mom! He wants me! Look, he's like glue. I can't get him off." Eventually, the baby was left by his tree and we went straight home to hot, soapy water. My life is crazier than fiction.

I asked Mr. Greer for today's schedule, and Evelyn immediately decided she wanted to attend school the entire day! "I think that may be overkill, Ev. I think you'll run out of energy." "Watch me!" That's honestly what she said to me! Her friend's dad once told the story of telling his wife that she should quit crying about Evelyn. "That girl's got moxie. I'm not worried about her. She'll be fine." I knew I had to let go and give her a chance to go to school all day. She wanted to be independent. After all, a normal return to everyday activities is our ultimate goal. I thought it was a wonderful problem to have—a child with a Traumatic Brain Injury insisting she return to school, but it made me feel vulnerable to let her out of my sight and send her into a school building. I told Evelyn to call me if she decided she needed to come home early.

We always walk to school, but it was raining this morning. As a favor, Jane picked up my kids to drive them for me. She saw my worried face as I stood in our front doorway. I walked Evelyn to Jane's van. She took my hand, calmly encouraged me that my daughter would be fine, and we shed a few happy, yet anxious tears about this important step for Evelyn. Jane had been in my shoes when Auggie returned to school after neurosurgery. He got to wear a hat, against school dress code, to cover the shaved section on his scalp. Jane understood this mother's heart and suggested I ask the nurse to check on Evelyn. I felt a terrible, jittery current of nervous energy, so antsy that it nearly made me physically ill.

That morning I sat behind my daughter at the All School Rosary and silently prayed, "Thank you, God. Thank you, God. Thank you, God!" Throughout the Rosary, I kept getting overwhelmed with emotion. Tears slid down my face. Sometimes intense emotions hit me like waves crashing into me, as though I'm walking toward the shore and get slammed forcefully from behind without warning.

The Hail Mary prayer is said over fifty times in the Catholic Rosary. I uttered the beginning of that prayer at the accident when my terror-stricken mind plummeted to the deepest, darkest, hell-on-earth truth that Evelyn could die in my arms. Those were heart-wrenching prayers. I said over and over, "I LOVE YOU, EVELYN! Stay awake. I'm here. Fight! Jesus loves you, Evelyn." Then I'd launch into the first line of the Hail Mary again. I got through the Rosary this morning, but it was absolutely emotionally exhausting.

After making face contact twice, Nurse Angela Carney called and said she thought Evelyn was annoyed with her. She has a sixth-grade daughter too, Norah, so she was understanding. I released the helpful nurse from her reconnaissance duty. She explained that Mrs. Jackie Buser, the PE teacher, had to make Evelyn stop trying to tag people during a gym class game. I had to breathe deeply as fear swelled within me upon receiving that report. At home before school, I told Evelyn in no uncertain terms that she was not cleared for any kind of physical activity yet, and she insisted, "I'm FINE." Although I felt frustrated with worry, it didn't surprise me much that Evelyn was pushing the envelope. It was another good problem to have, as opposed to the opposite outcome. That spunk was a huge part of her progress.

I headed to Sprouts, a nearby health-food store, to get fruit and some items to promote brain healing. At the checkout, Joseph, who ran the register, asked, "How is your morning going?" I sighed. I then gave him the three-sentence summary of my last three weeks and news of Evelyn returning to school today. I ended cheerfully, as though trying desperately to convince myself that life would indeed feel normal again, with, "So, I'm buying myself flowers!" He removed the cost of the bunch of gorgeous coral tulips from my bill and said, "These flowers are on me today." I burst into tears right then and there. It is such a joy to run into good people in life, especially when our hearts are most vulnerable. God wink.

I met my best friend from college, Nada, for a delicious First Watch brunch. We talked and laughed and vented and drank too much coffee. It was delightful and comforting to spend time with her. We always share without any filters, and such trust and openness are a blessing. It was a long-overdue visit, and so much had transpired. Our last visit was in the hospital on a very difficult day for Evelyn. Everything was exceptionally busy in our room, she felt terrible, and we barely had a moment to speak. I was exhausted and on edge. Time with my friend today was relaxing.

In an hour, my sixth grader will return home from her first full day of school, post-accident. Today marks three weeks since that fateful day. It is 2:31 PM, nearly the time that my life changed. I am more relaxed now than I was when I kissed Ev goodbye this morning. I am thankful for her determination and spirited character. She's such a blessing.

Chapter 22:
The Fighter

Last night our freshman daughter Olivia's Notre Dame de Sion track team gathered for an awards banquet. The invitation came during the chaos of our hospital stay, so I asked Robbie to handle the RSVP and dinner payment. I needed to find a friend to stay home with Evelyn, Henry, and Vivian while Robbie and I supported Olivia's strong track efforts through our attendance. Evelyn wanted to go, but I told her we had not RSVP'd and paid for her to attend. Kim Fiss, our next-door neighbor, came over to spend the evening with the kids. She was happy to have time to hang out and catch up with Evelyn, as they have developed a special friendship.

Olivia is a hard worker in all life endeavors, and running is her passion. Her spring shin injury caused frustration and was a setback. She saw a great physical therapist, Coach Amy Mitchell. Robbie researched and designed aqua-running and home-basement bike/strength/flexibility workouts to keep her in shape and strong while she rested her shin. Emily Finlason helped us access a pool for aqua-running rehab. In the end, Olivia came back strong in the 400 meters, and she was honored with some Personal Record awards last night. In her most recent race, she ran a 1:02 split for her leg of the 400 meters. We are very proud of the young woman Olivia is, and we respect her determination to overcome the obstacle of her injury. She has a district track meet tomorrow, racing in the open 400 meters and 4 x 400 meters relay. As I always yell, "GO O!"

At the end of the banquet the coaches passed engraved batons to the senior athletes. This tradition was inspired by a fine woman, Jennifer Waldenmeyer, who was friends with one of the current Sion coaches, Lori Donnelly. We all miss Jennifer since her passing. However, Jennifer's legacy remains in many ways, one of which is the track baton tradition.

As Coach Cody Buhrmeister began his explanation of the final award, his voice filling with emotion, he was forced to pause. He said he had a final baton to pass. He spoke about the baton as a symbol of life that represents the way we pass experiences on to one another. He said that the final baton was for Evelyn Overlease—The Fighter (at which point Robbie and I looked at one another totally stunned, and my eyes immediately filled with tears).

He explained her tragic accident of being struck by a falling tree limb. "It was very bad, but she has made a remarkable recovery. The baton is a gift from Sion so that Evelyn may pass on to others strength and inspiration from what she has been through."

Cody asked Robbie to receive the award on Evelyn's behalf. Olivia was crying. Jane and Chris Hill shared the joyous moment with us. It was amazing, touching, and unexpected! We felt so much love and support from another part of the body of our community, Notre Dame de Sion High School. We personally thanked the coaching staff after the event, and they compassionately spoke from their hearts when we visited individually. I hope Evelyn decides to run track under these fine coaches when she is a freshman and Olivia is a senior. Robbie and I have a happy fantasy of one day watching our daughters each run a leg of the 4 x 400 meters relay with Evelyn's extremely meaningful purple baton—a true symbol of perseverance and victory.

"Be on your guard, stand firm in the faith, be courageous, be strong. Your every act should be done with love." —1 Corinthians 16:13–14

Chapter 23

The Blue Bird of Hope

. . . . *Mother's Day, May 13, 2018*

I started my Mother's Day with Megan, my delightful sister-in-law, and my brother, Anthony—a fine grown man now, yet always a little brother to me. Anthony and Megan are visiting Kansas City because Megan's mother, Alice Ross, has been diagnosed with a metastatic brain mass. She is hospitalized while physicians seek to determine the primary source of cancer and plan neurosurgery. As my father would say, "We are not fortunate enough to have the luxury of dealing with only one crisis at a time."

We attended nine o'clock Mass, and upon entering the church an usher beelined for us to invite our family to be gift bearers of bread, water, wine, and collections. It was my honor to accept. The last time we were asked was Evelyn's first Sunday Mass after her accident. She felt extremely self-conscious about her shaved head, and her painful foot was bandaged in a boot. I declined that day out of respect for Evelyn's wishes and needs.

Today, Mother's Day, it brought me sheer joy to look around the church and see many friends (Emily, Amy, Nikki, Joanna, Shannon, Sarah, Jane, Katie, Laura, Allie, Christine, and others) who had been praying for my child and family. I knew they would see it as a blessing that the SIX of us were able to present the gifts to the altar for consecration by the priest on Mother's Day. It was special.

We felt doubly blessed that we were spared a terrible car accident last night on Highway 50 West on the way home from the Holden Sectionals

Track Meet in Missouri. Robbie and I drove separately due to conflicts with Vivian's soccer and Henry's baseball games. On the way home, Olivia and Evelyn rode with Robbie. I took "the littles," as I fondly refer to my youngest two children, in the minivan. Robbie led the way, but he pulled off to grab food for Olivia at a place where the rest of us had eaten lunch. I decided to go on without him, as the wait for lunch had been significant. Fifteen minutes later, my phone rang. Olivia, sobbing, said, "Mom, are you guys okay?!" Confused, I reassured her we were fine. I later found out that Robbie had come upon a wrecked white minivan, smoking—with the front end taken off.

A school bus from Grandview High School (track athletes) was lying on its side, and kids were scattered in the grass crying. Cars were pulled off to the sides of the road to assist, and Robbie had scanned them to search for my vehicle among the ones safely parked along the roadside without success. He told himself the white van was not mine. It simply couldn't be mine—not after the last three weeks we had faced. Olivia and Evelyn were terrified until Robbie spotted an unfamiliar decal on the window of the van. That was not our vehicle. Robbie exited to check on the people involved in the accident because emergency medical help had not yet arrived. He instructed Olivia to call 911. Luckily, there were no serious injuries. I was ahead of the wreck.

When the girls got home, Evelyn called out in search of me, then rushed straight into my arms, sobbing, "Mommy, I need a hug." She clung to me with all her might. "I'm so glad you're okay. I was mad at you (for not holding my backpack), and I felt awful when I thought the white van was yours. I don't want anything to ever happen to you. I was so scared." I wonder if she thought about the backyard accident and imagined my fear of losing her. We hugged one another tightly and took comfort in the love we felt.

After a nice Mother's Day breakfast prepared by Robbie with help from the kids, we decided to visit Alice Ross at St. Luke's Hospital in Kansas City. Evelyn had painted a card, written a nice note, and we prepared gifts to cheer Alice. Evelyn printed and framed a lovely sign for Alice that read, *"For God all things are possible."* —Matthew 19:26. I gave her a framed print of one of my favorite inspiring reminders, "Be joyful in hope, patient in affliction, faithful in prayer." The most special gift was the Blue Bird of Hope.

When Emily Finlason first visited Evelyn in the PICU, while Evelyn was still heavily sedated and intubated, Emily sat at the bedside, took my little girl's hand, and emotionally told this story.

"Evelyn, I have a special gift for you (as she unwrapped tissue paper). This is the Blue Bird of Hope, and my artist friend from Hallmark made it by hand for my mom (during her gastric cancer battle). Two days before Nana died she said with a slightly bossy tone, 'Emily, go get me that little bird! I don't need this bird anymore because I'm going to heaven to be with Jesus. You take this Blue Bird of Hope and save it for someone who's going to need it.'"

With that, Emily gave it to Evelyn. You can imagine the surge of emotion that Robbie, Emily, and I felt at that moment. Yesterday, my big-hearted young daughter asked me what I thought she should do with her Blue Bird of Hope. "Do you think it would be okay to give it to Alice?" With Emily's kind blessing, even though she may have hoped to pass it to her close friend Brenda, a young mom fighting breast cancer, Evelyn passed the gift of the Blue Bird of Hope forward to Alice. All the adults in the hospital room felt emotion well up within them as I shared the story.

Evelyn has always been wise beyond her years. She wants the gift of the Blue Bird of Hope to provide comfort to Alice during her time of waiting to learn a diagnosis and prognosis. Hope on! I see this as an additional good that has come from Evelyn's accident. Hope abounds. God's goodness has been revealed in countless ways through the course of Evelyn's interactions with others. It is truly astounding. The hand of God is always upon us.

"Is anyone among you suffering? He should pray." —James 5:13

Chapter 24

Half Full

Divine providence is a curious thing. We didn't miss the God wink when we realized that the husband, Pablo Aguayo, of the couple we've become friends with from Olivia's high school was Head of Trauma at CMH. Dr. Aguayo made rounds on Evelyn in the hospital and brought her balloons. Some would call his involvement a random occurrence, but I think otherwise. It is more likely that our connection was perfectly orchestrated by God's timing. I didn't know which physician Evelyn would see for her Trauma/Surgery Team follow-up appointment three weeks post-op, but it was Pablo.

Pablo's wife, Elizabeth, intended to pray a Seven Sorrows of Mary Servite Rosary with us at Evelyn's hospital bedside on Thursday, April 27; but the steady stream of therapists and consults, and a multitude of appreciated, yet unexpected visitors, prevented her kind plan from reaching fruition. Elizabeth chose the gift of the Servite Rosary because of the hopeful promises for those who use this special Rosary in devotion to Mary, including granting peace to their families and consoling them in their pain. The meditations focus on the sorrows that Mary the Virgin Mother of God compassionately endured during the suffering and death of Jesus, her Divine Son. My friend's gift was considerate and relevant, and it reminded me to maintain proper perspective. Evelyn and I suffered, but certainly not to the degree of Christ and Mary. Everything is relative.

Evelyn's second appointment was scheduled over an hour later, with Rehabilitation Medicine. It was another gorgeous, cloudless, blue-sky day with chirping birds. My daughter and I laughed and ate yummy sandwiches outside on the same bench where we were reunited with Winston. She wore my sunglasses, and after finishing her food, she stretched out her long limbs in the sunshine on a bench to soak up some warmth while I made another dent in thank-you-note writing.

It was nice to see the faces of the impressive Rehabilitation Medicine team again. Most noteworthy, one by one, therapists and nurses laid eyes on my daughter and absolutely lit up at the sight of such a pretty, bright-eyed, healthy child who came through an awful accident with restored health and vitality. She was in bad shape when members of the medical team first met Evelyn, and her recovery was astounding to one and all. Children are resilient and amazing, but our Evelyn was irrepressible. The reactions of the health-care providers brought me elation and feelings of utter gladness!

Evelyn saw her favorite hospital employee, Kelly from Occupational Therapy. Her strength and ability to maneuver her fingers, on her left side especially, earned a great report. The physical therapist was satisfied with Evelyn's overall body strength and balance. The speech pathologist gave Evelyn a repeat of some tests from the hospital. Evelyn was asked to name as many animals as she could think of in one minute. She had to spout off a list of words beginning with the letter M, without using proper nouns, for one minute. She started off strong, but after the 40-second mark, there was utter silence.

When we discussed what was happening in Evelyn's brain as she attempted to recall the requested information, the answer was that she simply went totally blank. Dr. Korth, an expert neuropsychologist, explained that Evelyn was basically accessing a mental file box of animals. She thought of a category, such as barn animals or animals around our home, and she listed them. After she recalled additional categories, she hit a point where the file folders she flipped through during the exercise simply ended. There were no more files. She could not think of one more animal no matter how hard she tried. Although this was unsettling to me, it is a normal outcome for a patient with a moderate to severe Traumatic Brain Injury (TBI). It signified that the brain still had healing to do, and that process takes many months to get back to normal.

Dr. Korth told Evelyn that she was going to administer a computer test to measure her reaction time, processing speed, and memory. She said it would take twenty minutes, and I should move to the waiting room. Evelyn did not anticipate any testing, and she was not thrilled with the notion. Not one bit. I thought it was fantastic that we would leave the appointment with some data to indicate Evelyn's level of brain healing. Dr. Korth wanted Evelyn to be fast and accurate with her test results, and she scored within the expected range of "normal." However, this test also showed that her brain needed more time to heal, which made sense to the doctor based on the severity of Evelyn's head injury. I also had to chuckle when Evelyn disclosed that she was reprimanded for starting the test before completely reading the directions on how to take it. Ev said the screen had "too many words, so I just skipped it." Impulsive. Lack of impulse control was a possible outcome of TBI, and right out of the gate Evelyn demonstrated that that was something she must work to improve.

What caught us off guard in the appointment with Dr. Vargas, another member of the team, was his line of questioning regarding Evelyn's resuming physical activities. Where the neurosurgeon expressed a "take it easy for a couple of months" attitude, the rehabilitation physicians were adamant about a recommendation that Evelyn sit out of contact sports for a full year. No one had previously mentioned such a restraint, so although it should have occurred to us previously, it was a bit shocking and felt like bad news.

Evelyn plays on a recreational soccer league team with great friends, and she isn't shy on the field. Dr. Kim Hartman explained that for girls, soccer is the sport with the highest rate of concussions. Although a broken ankle can be fixed with a cast and healed with time, it is harder to protect and heal the brain. A second injury to Evelyn's brain could result in a significantly more difficult recovery course. She was so blessed with an amazing recovery after her accident that it makes no sense to risk long-term learning/brain issues by allowing her to jump back into her previous contact sports.

Basketball, which the doctors described as a gray area in terms of "contact sport" status, is Evelyn's new love. She was asked by the sixth-grade coach, Tim Murphy, the dad of Ev's friend Lauryn, to join the team with Maggie in order for there to be enough girls to form a viable team. She took to the sport, excelled, and thoroughly enjoyed it. However, Robbie and I will not allow Evelyn to play basketball on the school team in the winter. She's little, but she is an effective rebounder! Taking an elbow to the top of the head is too risky. She's going to fight us on our decision, and I understand how sad she will feel to sit out of a team sport that truly brought her incredible enjoyment and lit the fire of her competitive nature.

When we consider the big picture and long-term benefit to laying off sports for a year, it is a no-brainer, no pun intended. My nurse friend and mother of six, Joanna Nickson, said, "Head injuries have such a long recovery, and better to completely heal than run any risk of re-injury. Her recovery is most definitely fantastic!" She's right. We all understand how fortunate Evelyn is to have a foot, an intact spine, her sight . . . her LIFE. Such outcomes could have kept Evelyn out of sports for a lifetime. However, it is human nature to desire more. I hate that my active, determined, adolescent girl must hold back from activities that bring her good health, social camaraderie, and childhood fun.

Evelyn's friend's mom and I texted about the news. "I know it will be super hard for Ev for the social and physical part of it. Not even the organized sports, but the rough-and-tumble play like trampoline, bike riding, diving board, running around as they know it during play. When even what seems like the 'ordinary' is restricted, that is super hard. I sense some new hobbies coming on." Kind friends and family have wisely suggested that God opens doors when others close. Maybe this is a time for her to explore new interests and hobbies, sewing or painting, golf or tennis. We'll trust in his plan, and we know that a year will speed past us since we know time flies. We will keep our eyes on the blessings that abound in Evelyn's life right now. We will strive to see the situation in "half-full" light. Our associate priest, Fr. Justin, suggested that Evelyn's "sports sacrifice" will build character and virtue.

What my naturally athletic little girl once took for granted as her norm, running and playing hard in whatever sport she selected, she now recognizes as a privilege and a gift. Upon re-entry to such athletic endeavors, I know she will approach sports opportunities with a heart full of gratitude. "Say YES to new adventures," and "Good things take time," are fitting reminders. How wise Evelyn's sisters were when they selected such meaningful and relevant quotes for their mama's book of inspiration.

"May the Lord of peace himself give you peace at all times and in every way."
—2 Thessalonians 3:16

Chapter 25:
The Beauty of Her Left Side

‿‿‿

The June day that I watched Evelyn's tennis lesson at Overland Park Racquet Club I dissolved into tears (I know, I know—so much crying) by the depth of my gratitude for her wonderful healing. We saw tennis as a perfect new athletic pursuit for her: a noncontact, yet active, lifelong sport. Close to the net, Evelyn's twenty-something, private instructor from the United Kingdom, David Fox, led her through a rapid volley drill in which she returned a volley, caught a tennis ball in her left hand, tossed it back to him, and got ready for another ball headed her way. She was fluid. Her left hand's manual dexterity, and her eye-hand coordination, speed, and agility caused big tear droplets to blur my vision, spill over, and slide down my face.

Images of Evelyn immobile and barely able to open her eye (the other one was black and swollen shut!) from weakness filled my head. Again and again, doctors did neurological checks in which she reported that she could not feel her left arm. The anguish that such exams caused this mother's heart was extraordinary. It took a few days post op in the PICU before Evelyn could move her fingers or toes on the left side AT ALL!

Decked out in stylish tennis clothes from Athleta, a gift from Grandma Mary and Grandpa Mike, Ev sported an *I Dream of Jeannie* ultra-high ponytail and played tennis like she wasn't brand new to the sport. Her emergency neurosurgery had occurred a month and a half prior. Amazing! I was so, SOOO happy that Evelyn was healthy and strong.

Even though time has passed, sometimes everything related to Evelyn's accident still seems so fresh. I feel so vulnerable. I constantly worry about an accident befalling Robbie or one of our other active children. There are things that get me every time, such as seeing the red leash Winston was wearing on our neighborhood walk right before the accident. I should probably just put it away! Other times, I will begin to text someone, and I'll notice my friend's last communication was a heartfelt offer of prayers and support late in the evening on April 20.

The day of the accident was the most difficult day Robbie and I have ever experienced. Late that evening we were physically and emotionally exhausted. We waited hours during surgery; gazed upon our intubated little girl; viewed her shaved head and wounded, injured foot. We waited on pins and needles for Evelyn to wake up from her anesthesia. Every single thing was an unknown. We had prayers, love, and support from family and friends, and each other. We had our dear Evelyn—alive. That was a start.

We didn't know what version of Evelyn awaited us. We chose faith over fear, as best we could. We love our children unconditionally, No Matter What. However, I believe it is human nature and quite normal to desire a smooth road for our beloved children, as opposed to a rocky, steep, mountain of a climb in life. From the moment Evelyn opened her eye and recognized us, we felt more secure about the state of her mind and future.

Unfortunately, Evelyn was at the beginning of her walk of suffering. One practical part of life that helps us get through the worst of times is that we only experience life a moment at a time. Often in life, if we knew ahead of time all the trials and awful struggles we would be forced to face over an expanse of our future, we couldn't handle it. We wouldn't feel strong, equipped, or courageous enough to go forward. The truth would paralyze us. However, we just take a step, then another step, and onward we move through life. I think that is a key to handling adversity. We are not well served by trying to get too far ahead in our thinking.

Sometimes, it is more advantageous to simply live in the moment and take what comes a bit at a time. Bible study ladies have encouraged, "Just take the next good step." *We are not in control.* If we turn to Scripture, it will shape our perspective and remind us of our Divine Master's plan for our ultimate good; for we are not self-sufficient. Thus, our acceptance of our dependence upon God is an attitude to embrace. We need God. These are practical words of wisdom, but living their message is exceptionally challenging. If we remain mindful of our heart's desire to trust God's holy will, and we believe that we may not rely upon ourselves, but must find strength in the Lord, then we have a chance. As a middle-school teacher and then as a parent, I set the expectations bar high. We must aim for our baseline mindset to be a "trust in God" approach that we may amp up in times of trouble. "Shoot for the moon. Even if you miss, you'll land among the stars." —Norman Vincent Peale

"Therefore do not worry about tomorrow, for tomorrow will worry about itself. Each day has enough trouble of its own." —Matthew 6:34 (NIV)

Chapter 26

I Promise to Stand by You

Jenny McGinnis, a friend from Curé, put songs on two music CDs (one upbeat and inspirational and the other calming and encouraging) for Evelyn at my request. Jenny loves music, and I knew she would compile a selection of songs certain to inspire my music-loving daughter and cheer her up during her recovery. Evelyn is known for blaring her music upstairs as she sings boldly. It is a delight to experience the joy that music brings to the human heart. "Scars," "broken," "tears," "hurt"—we understand those words in a song by Rachel Platten, "Stand by You." You should look it up and play it. The message will give you hope in your direst situations.

The words of that song were our words. Evelyn owned them. When this song plays in our minivan I always reach out and take my darling Evelyn's hand and I sing. The songwriter vividly depicts my true attitude toward supporting my children, my friends, and those I love who must deal with hard times. We love one another, and we will stand together and hold each other up no matter what.

When the Hills' adolescent son, Auggie, was involved in a hit-and-run accident while biking in the crosswalk in front of our church and school, everything that happened on April 20 rushed back to me with the force of a punch to the gut. I found myself sweating and shaking at the scene of the accident as I spoke to paramedics and the police before Auggie's parents' arrival on the scene. Ultimately, Jane and Chris, and the rest of us, felt extremely thankful for such a positive outcome. Auggie suffered some abrasions, but escaped a devastating head injury or broken bones.

It also added another layer of mother-to-mother empathy, love, and strength to my relationship with Jane. Auggie's accident reinforced the notion that we are totally helpless to protect our loved ones at all times, and it makes us feel especially insecure. An old friend recently expressed this sentiment as, "This love business makes us so agonizingly vulnerable."

Sometimes bad things happen. This is a harsh fact of life. We are left with little choice but to trust God. Worrying does nothing. Matthew 6:27 reminds us, *"And who of you by being worried can add a single hour to his life?"* What will be, will be.

A worrier by nature, I truly struggle with this matter. The words of Fr. Jacques Philippe in his treatise on peace of heart provide sound advice: "Happy are those whose hearts are purified by faith and hope, who bring to their lives a view animated by the certitude that, beyond appearances to the contrary, God is present, providing for their essential needs, and that they lack nothing. If they have that faith, they will indeed see God: they will experience that presence of God which will accompany them and guide them. They will see that many of the circumstances that they thought negative and damaging to their spiritual life are, in fact, in God's pedagogy, powerful means for helping them to progress and grow." In other words, there is a rich opportunity to seek the silver lining and to develop stronger faith when we must face the challenges that are inescapable in life.

In my Bible study, we have discussed that although suffering and facing challenges we encounter in life are extremely difficult, sometimes we arrive at a point and learn a lesson that we could gain in no other way than by going through our trial, rather than over or around it. There are things we learn through adversity that we can't learn any other way. We don't choose, we don't like, and we can't change the crosses we must bear. We must keep praying and remember that God is in control. We should strive to be steadfast believers, accepting his will, and trusting his wisdom and love. I find the following prayer a tremendously hopeful reminder. It offers quite a promise for our ultimate goodness and peace.

Trust in God
by St. Francis de Sales

Do not look forward to the trials and crosses of this life with dread and fear.

Rather, look to them with full confidence that, as they arise, God, to whom you belong, will deliver you from them.

He has guided and guarded you thus far in life.

Do you but hold fast to His dear hand, and He will lead you safely through all trials.

Whenever you cannot stand, He will carry you lovingly in His arms.

Do not look forward to what may happen tomorrow.

The same Eternal Father who cares for you today will take care of you tomorrow and every day of your life.

Either He will shield you from suffering or He will give you the unfailing strength to bear it.

Be at peace then and put aside all useless thoughts, vain dreads, and anxious imaginations.

"[P]repare yourself for trials. Be sincere of heart and steadfast, undisturbed in time of adversity. Cling to him, forsake him not; thus will your future be great. Accept whatever befalls you, in crushing misfortune be patient; for in fire gold is tested. . . . Trust God and he will help you; make straight your ways and hope in him." —Sirach 2:1–6

Chapter 27

Mountains to Climb

On Monday, July 16, 2018, Evelyn competed in a doubles tennis match with one of her closest friends, Anna Gillespie, a fellow Prairie Village Junior Tennis League teammate and longtime classmate. Anna was on the web swing with another girl at the Goodmans' house when the limb broke. She visited Ev in the hospital and at our home and provided true friendship and great comfort during her recovery. Knowing how mortified Evelyn felt about her shaved head, Anna and other friends empathetically gave her the tremendously practical gift of a monogrammed, light-blue baseball cap. With the support of her mother, my kind friend Leann, Anna happily joined Evelyn in her new pursuit of tennis this summer; this made the activity much more attractive to my ultra-social daughter. The girls did not win their match, but they gained valuable experience—about nuances in the game of tennis and the art of negotiating line calls and the score with other players. Life lessons abounded!

Physically, Evelyn's long blonde hair boasts highlights from a summer spent playing tennis on sunny courts and swimming at the pool with friends and siblings. Her skin is sun kissed, her muscles long and lean. She's a truly beautiful young lady and always displays a "go-getter, get after it" attitude on the tennis court. It is fun to watch her play, even though she is a beginner. If my little girl were a famous rapper, I would suggest she call herself Tenacious E. It fits. Evelyn's Aunt Andrea thinks of her tough niece when she hears "*Titanium*" by David Guetta with a line about determination and strength. The multiple titanium microplates in Evelyn's skull give her a certain bulletproof quality in line with her indomitable nature.

Twice in the last week I've had to explain to Dr. Wilcoxon, our orthodontist, and Dr. Winburn, our family dentist, prior to Evelyn's exams, that she was involved in a serious accident and suffered a TBI and a mandible fracture. When Robbie and I look at Evelyn now, we marvel at our child's healthy appearance and good medical status. When I reflect on the difficulties she faced and overcame, it seems incomprehensible that Evelyn was so badly injured, so weak and filled with pain, yet today is in such fine shape. I am left with the impression that Evelyn's outcome was touched by the divine. The hand of God was upon her. People call her our little miracle. Her younger sister said she's only two miracles away from becoming a saint, and this brought on many smiles.

I sat in our church on our eighteenth wedding anniversary, July 1, 2018, and tears fell during the gospel (Mark 5:21–43) account of the gravely ill twelve-year-old girl, the daughter of Jairus. When her father approached Jesus and asked for help, Jesus said, "Do not be afraid. Just have faith" (v. 36). Before Jesus was able to go to the girl, they received news of her death. However, we find hope in Mark 5:40–42: "He took along the child's father and mother and those who were with him and entered the room where the child was. He took the child by the hand and said to her, 'Talitha koum,' which means, 'Little girl, I say to you, arise!' The child arose immediately and walked around. At that they were utterly astounded." Jesus was all-powerful over death. He saved the child. He saved my child.

Our sweet, faith-filled, creative, headstrong, and all-things-bright-and-beautiful little girl was on death's door in the yard of her friend at the accident. We all feared. Those present in the yard, her closest friends, mom, dad, grandpa, grandma, friends' mothers—we feared Evelyn's young life would be lost at any moment. Death was pounding at the door. Unfortunately, given the height from which the large tree limb fell with significant mass and the great force of nature, that was a realistic, terrible possibility.

We also had faith. What could we do but pray and hope? The book of Romans reminds us that everything depends on faith and everything is grace.

Our family's fate was always in God's hands after the accident, and good came of our devastating ordeal. One of the coleaders of my Bible study, JoAnn LaBarge, a devout Catholic woman filled with an encyclopedic wealth of scriptural knowledge, wrote me after she read my first detailed update. JoAnn thanked me for sharing Evelyn's journey, and she offered, "Years ago, a rabbi wrote a book entitled *Why Do Bad Things Happen to Good People?* It has been said that a better title would be *What Happens to Good People When Bad Things Happen to Them?* You have answered that last question fully in your email update—blessings, grace, and healing are flowing from the Lord's throne into your lives!! Thank you for sharing those blessings with us (as well as your tears). God bless."

Katie read *Life of the Beloved* by Henri Nouwen and shared some excerpts from his work that spoke about our "brokenness," which the priest author equates to our suffering in life, while we were in the hospital. She understood through hospital visits and brutally honest communications with me the all-encompassing pain, through her whole little body, that Evelyn endured. For long stretches, nothing alleviated Evelyn's pain. It enveloped her. Evelyn complained of relentless head pain, and her hurt weighed on my mind and saddened my heart. I longed to take the pain from Evelyn, yet I was powerless to do so.

Nouwen wrote, "Suffering—be it physical, mental, or emotional—is almost always experienced as an unwelcome intrusion into our lives, something that should not be there. It is difficult, if not impossible, to see anything positive in suffering; it must be avoided at all costs." He further reflected upon the importance of trusting in our strength to stand our suffering and being able to "grow strong through it."

Katie offered in a letter, "Not sure if the suffering will start seeming like a burden and questions about 'why' will settle in, but perhaps some of these words will help you and Robbie and Ev along the way. This will be such a big part of Evelyn's story and journey for the rest of her life. I know she'll make the most of it."

Evelyn has experienced "why" moments. She has been brought to sobs about WHY the top of her head had to be shaved in such a large patch and how many years it may take to grow back to full length when the average person's hair grows a measly half-inch per month. "WHY did that tree have to fall on my head?" she has angrily demanded to have answered. Evelyn has contemplated the why. We get it! Evelyn is a child, and her perspective is not yet that of an adult.

Evelyn, good will come of your accident. Good has come of your accident! We have been blessed with a community of faith in action—praying, loving and supporting us in myriad meaningful ways. We have been disciplined in the value of trusting in the Lord's holy will, leaning on Jesus with total and complete trust in difficult times. I hope that as my daughter matures in age and grows in faith throughout her lifetime, her perspective on this stretch of her life will shift. She will see the outcome of her accident through the lens of an adult's perspective. She will recall all the ways her experience impacted other people. I pray that Evelyn will take to heart and feel the blessing of her healing that was realized in the prayer, so powerful in its simple reminder, of Don Dolindo Ruotolo in his *Novena of Surrender to the Will of God*, "Oh Jesus, I surrender myself to you, take care of everything!" He will. We must trust his goodness.

When our hearts are open to the whisper of God, he speaks words of encouragement to our souls and fuels the flame of our faith, and this sustains us. We are able to see the stars, the beauty of the light of Christ, even in the midst of the deep and consuming darkness. We may seek and find meaning in our suffering. "The wilderness will lead you to your heart where I will speak," is a line from *Hosea* by Gregory Norbet, with which I sincerely connect. Difficult stretches in life form us.

Faith is a gift that has been bestowed upon us, and I can't live without it any more than I would be able to live without a backbone, heart, or brain. My faith is essential to my being and of paramount importance in my life, and I pray for people who must get through times of intense difficulty without faith. God's love and grace is for them too.

The Holy Spirit is ready to slip into open hearts to fill them with love, grace, and peace. Walking the winding and hilly road of the last months with family members and friends united in faith, hope, love, and prayer has strengthened and blessed us immeasurably. We are not alone. We have each other, and our Almighty God is always with us. "God's power is unleashed when God's people pray." —Max Lucado

In the aftermath, my heart yearns to discover nuggets of goodness that emerged from our tragic and miraculous event to seek meaning in the trials. Sometimes circumstances shake us up in a way that causes us to run to God. I know a man in his sixties who does not speak about belief in God. Upon learning the grave news of Evelyn's condition immediately following the accident, he rushed to and knelt before a photo of his beloved, deceased mother. Filled with raw emotion, he called out to her and implored her and her sister, angels as he saw them, to race to Evelyn's aid if they could hear him. Later, after it became clear that Evelyn's young life had been spared, this man shared his experience with a family member and spoke the most wonderful words: "I guess I do believe."

Through the harm that came to Evelyn the soul of a man encountered God's might and grace, and he believed. Disbelief turned to renewed faith. This is utterly beautiful. It is profound in the magnitude of its importance, and it blesses my heart that his private and beautiful story was made known to me.

Our young associate pastor, Fr. Justin Hamilton, shared a touching homily on July 15, 2018. He articulated a perspective that I want Evelyn to believe when she contemplates her accident:

Everything we encounter in life is exactly what God knows is best for us, no matter how disagreeable or hard it is to embrace. That's not at all to say that some things, like losing a loved one, dealing with a chronic illness, or losing one's job are objectively good things. Rather, God is able to take painful, challenging events like this and apply them to our lives in such a way that they are transformed into the very best thing for us, the catalyst for the deepest growth, the best way to purify our love and sharpen our faith, if only we would embrace them just like He embraced His cross. The key to this is finding God in these moments, knowing that He is always present in our lives, if only we look for Him and ask Him to reveal Himself.

I see God all around us. I see God in the smiling faces of our dear children and in the compassionate expressions of loving relatives and friends. I feel God deeply during many beautiful moments rich in thousands of years of tradition in our Catholic Mass and in the uplifting lyrics of hymns. I have stood spellbound in the stunningly magnificent cathedrals of Europe, erected over great expanses of time to honor our supreme Maker. However, in my lifetime, I have experienced no place on earth where God's majesty is more evident than the splendor of the mountains.

On July 28, 2018, our family arrived in Frisco, Colorado, for a vacation in Summit County. Due to Evelyn's Traumatic Brain Injury, Robbie and I knew that we must tone down our outdoor activities to protect our child from another head injury. White-water rafting, mountain biking, alpine amusement parks, and mountain climbing were out. My dear husband has a streak of adventure within his core, and he's the parent who always lets the kids take things a bit past my conservative level of comfort. I am risk averse and Robbie likes an occasional thrill. I told the kids that this summer we would take walks in the woods, not steep mountain hikes like last summer.

Robbie is a protective father who does extensive research in every pursuit. However, he selected a hike for our family that he may have conveniently decided NOT to tell me was rated "Difficult" by USNFS standards until AFTER we completed the hike. He didn't share with me that the Mount Royal/Masontown hike had an elevation gain of 1,372 feet over two miles to the 10,482-foot summit. Nor did he share the line from the hike's description that stated, "This hike is considered a mountain replacement for a 'Stair Stepper' machine and involves loose rock. Hiking poles would definitely come in handy on this hike."

We set out with our four children in our running shoes from the prior school year . . . all with worn tread! Robbie was our fearless leader. I carried a backpack loaded down with our jackets and six water bottles! Robbie carried lunch for the family. The kids—young and fast and healthy and strong—just hiked. Our calves burned. Our hearts pounded. Our chests heaved. Everyone we passed coming down the trail—and they were all adults—had hiking poles. That got my attention. We breathed hard, yet upward we climbed. More than once, in the name of safety and with a protective mother's voice of reason, I had to ask Evelyn to stop leaping off the trail to click her heels in midair sideways, celebration style.

After two hours of climbing we reached the summit of Mount Royal. We looked out over the land below. The sight was breathtakingly beautiful. We were on top of the world—in physical altitude and with emotional elation and a sense of accomplishment.

Evelyn hopped upon a section of rock and happily called out, "Hey, Mom! Take my picture," as she flashed a big smile and struck a mighty pose with fists on her hips and one foot placed upon a higher section of the mountain as though she owned it.

My heart just about burst with happiness. I shared the stunning photo of Evelyn with her pediatrician since she was a baby, Natasha Burgert, MD, with the note, "This sums up the joy in my heart over Evelyn's recovery from April 20. Praise God!" Natasha responded, "Powerful. Beautiful. Confident. This photo makes my WEEK! So happy and full of praise."

Blessed Pier Giorgio Frassati was constantly striving to reach the blessings of eternal life through the actions he took and sacrifices he made on Earth to serve the poor. The words *Verso L'alto* ("to the heights") were penned by him on a photo taken a month before his unexpected death. In the photo, the twenty-four-year-old was climbing a mountain and looking skyward. The translation conveys that the higher we go, the better we may hear the voice of Christ. I heard a great, holy "Alleluia!" the day that Evelyn climbed Mount Royal. God was there, smiling down upon us, delighting in our great joy, rejoicing with our family. What a magical moment!

Our adolescent daughter suffered from the impact of a tree limb crashing onto her head. Her life was impacted in that moment, and our perspective was forever altered. Evelyn picked up a chunk of wood from the tree that harmed her when we revisited the yard. She kept it hidden away in her bedroom until she brought it to me one day with the words, "Cherish each day like it's your last," penned in her own hand. The accident with the tree changed Evelyn's life.

184 • *Hope Upon Impact*

Evelyn now values the gift of her life in a way uncanny for a child; and although we should all live with this profound truth as our outlook, as her mother I find it indeed hurts my inner being that Evelyn's sense of security was so deeply shaken. She lives boldly and fearlessly, for which I admire and envy her, but the fragility of life is present in the back of her mind. Our family, friends, and community were impacted by her improbable and tragic accident. However, with the fervent prayers and blessings of a faith-filled, loving, wide circle of support; the marvels of modern medicine at a leading-edge children's hospital; Evelyn's inner strength, drive, and tremendous grit; and the power of God, Evelyn's story has the happiest ending imaginable.

My daughter climbed a mountain. Do you hear me?!

MY DAUGHTER CLIMBED A MOUNTAIN.

And, she isn't finished yet. She's got more mountains to climb.

Watch her.

Thank you, dear God.

"[L]et me sing of the Lord, 'He has been good to me.'" —Psalm 13:6

Appendix

The CT of Evelyn's head/brain, taken at 3:30 PM on April 20 yielded the following impressions.

1. Complex fracture of the left superior orbit/left frontal bone and diastases of the left frontal suture with subjacent thin subdural hemorrhage. No substantial mass effect on the adjacent brain.

2. Complex fracture of the right parietal bone with a 5 mm depression of a 5 cm plate of the mid-parietal bone. Equivocal extension of a posterior inferolateral margin of inner table into the adjacent frontoparietal brain. Minimal adjacent extra-axial hemorrhage, without mass effect.

3. Minimal right superior para midline frontal subarachnoid hemorrhage.

The CT Maxillofacial showed this:

1. Left orbital roof and left lateral orbital wall fractures with adjacent left periorbital and lacrimal gland swelling and mild edema/hemorrhage in the superior and superolateral left extraconal orbit with mild inferior displacement of the superior rectus muscle.

2. Left lateral frontal parietal fractures and left frontal suture diastases as detailed above and in the head CT report.

3. Minimal diastases of the left frontal sphenoidal, left temporal sphenoidal, and left petro occipital synchondrosis.

4. Nondisplaced fracture in the left sphenoid bone extending through the foramen ovale and probably into the lateral wall of the left petrous carotid canal.

5. Equivocal fracture into the medial right superior carotid canal versus variant anatomy of the spheno-occipital synchondrosis.

6. Right mid-mandibular condylar fracture.

Critical results: Trauma surgery resident Jason was notified of the probable involvement of the carotid canals, and CT angiography was recommended at 5:00 PM 4/20/2018.

Questions from Mom with Reflections
by Evelyn

What is the last thing you remember from Friday, April 20, 2018?

I remember playing tennis with my friends. It was a nice, sunny day, and Mrs. Goodman walked out with a piping-hot plate of pizza. We all swarmed the plate, and the pizza was gone in a flash. I bit into the pizza, and it burned my tongue. I set the plate down and waited for it to cool down, then my memory goes blank. I don't know what day the bits and pieces of my memory from the hospital are from, but I do remember being rushed through the hallway on a rolling bed. I looked around very confused, and I saw my mom with trickles of tears running down her cheeks. I shut my eyes, and my next memory was being put into a long white tube that I suppose was an MRI. I looked around, and then the memory goes blank again.

What were the greatest challenges you faced in the hospital? Physically? Emotionally?

After all this happened there were many challenges that I faced. Emotionally, the problem I faced was my hair or the hair I didn't even have. When my head was first shaved in the hospital I had no idea because I never even got up out of bed. When I had to go to the bathroom I had a tube that let me pee—GROSS. Oh, and I had a bedpan. When I was finally able to walk and get out of bed I had to walk to the bathroom with my IV tubes connected to a cart. Once I got there it definitely didn't feel like home. There was cream tile up and down the walls with a colored stripe of tile around the bathroom. I walked in to use the restroom. When I was done I walked to the sink with my head down. As I looked up to get soap I saw my face in the mirror. At first I just stared at my face. I had a huge black eye, a very swollen face, and worst of all—a shaved head! After I ran everything through my head my eyes started tearing up, and then out the tears came. I was so sad and mad at the same time. I was downright hideous. I hated looking at my shaved head with the scars on it. Still today, when I see my shaved head in the mirror it feels unreal, but in the end it is just my battle scar.

Physically, it was hard getting around because my foot was hurt and my left side was weak. I remember walking through the hospital hallway holding onto my physical therapist's arm. I had a braid in my hair, and as I walked by I saw people working on their computers. I was hoping none of them looked up to see my ugly shaved head, but they did, and they gave me a warm smile. Even four months later when I'm putting my hair up in a ponytail for tennis or when I'm swimming, and all the short hair pokes though, I get so frustrated. I look in the mirror and just think, "Why?! Why did all this happen? Why won't my hair just cooperate? WHY?"

Now that I think about it, maybe the reason why is because every time I see my hair or try to hide the short parts I think of the accident. Maybe instead of being angry I should think of all the people that prayed for me, the ones I didn't even know, how my community gave me gifts and made my family dinner, how my class made me a funny get-well video and gave me tons of cards. Maybe my hair is supposed to be a reminder of how many people love me and care.

What do you remember and how did you feel about the neurological checks in the hospital when the doctors asked you if you could move your left-side limbs and extremities (and you couldn't)?

I don't remember anything related to that.

What brought you the most comfort during your hospital stay?

What brought me the most comfort was definitely my mom. She was with me every single night and slept on the most uncomfortable bed you could imagine just to be with me. She did anything I wanted, like pulling my covers up or even helping me get up from the toilet. My mom was there for me the whole time, and she still is. I love her so much.

My family and friends helped, too. Maggie Axtell, one of my really close friends, visited me right after it happened and a few other times too. Seeing her come more than once just to see me was so kind and made me feel loved. She would come and we would talk while our parents were outside the room. She told me about school and what all was going on, and she made me laugh, which I hadn't done since she came. About four months after I got home from the hospital I was at her house, and as we drove home Maggie handed me a piece of the branch from the tree from the Goodmans' yard that had loving and encouraging words written all over it. When I got home and showed my mom, she cried and gave me a big hug. I put it on my dresser and it's still there. Every night I look up at it and just smile knowing that I really do have a true friend.

Why were you so resistant to taking any medication to decrease your headache and foot pain once you left the hospital?

At first glance I just answered, "I don't like medicine," to this question, but that isn't entirely true. Now sure, it's not like I enjoyed taking medicine, but I did take it at times when I had the option; like if I had a headache I would take it. During my stay at the hospital, well, they gave me medicine like it was a sport. All day every day something would be going into me. It might not have always been medicine, but there was something going into me by a tube. When I had all the tubes in I didn't mind it as much because I couldn't taste it. Although I didn't taste anything, I felt something, a cold feeling going down my throat. Closer to the day I was released, I had to show that I could eat on my own, or I had to keep the feeding tube. That included taking the medicine by mouth, through my throat, and tasting it. I guess the medicine was "flavored," but it did not help at all. If anything, it made the taste even worse. I got so tired of the medicine. It was constant, and after I got out of the hospital I was done with medicine. I didn't ever want to take it again—until I found out that I still had to take it at home.

There were two types. I had to take them both three times a day, I recall. So that's six times. The kind I was taking wasn't just normal. It was horrible. It was as if they tried to make it the grossest taste ever. I had to take two teaspoons of it, so we put it in Shatto chocolate milk to hide the bad taste. Now I don't want to drink chocolate milk anymore because it reminds me of the medicine ordeal. Once I was done with that after a week, I was extra done with medicine.

So yeah, I'd rather have some pain than take some horrible medicine. You may be thinking, Why not just take a pill? Well, that's a long story;

let's just say I can't swallow pills. Unless they are almost microscopic and coated, I can't take it, and most times the pill is not that small. That's why I don't take medicine anymore. I think the hospital has already given me enough for a lifetime.

Share your thoughts about the long scar on the top of your right foot.

My thought on my scar is that it is just a battle scar. When I'm older and I meet new people I can just make up a story like a shark bit me or something cooler than *a tree ripped up my foot*. I like having a scar that shows what I've been through. I don't care that it's raised or bumpy or even purple. My scar is my own version of a mood ring, only it adjusts to my body temperature. It changes color based on my temperature. If I'm freezing cold, it is purple. If I am room temperature, it is flesh colored. It's my foot, and I like it just the way it is.

Why do you think your body and brain have recovered so quickly and fully?

I think I have recovered so quickly because so many people prayed for me. My classmates, friends, parents, relatives, siblings, and even people I don't even know or have never met prayed. Some people that don't even live in the same country as me said prayers.

How do you think your personality helped you handle difficulties after the accident?

I think my personality has helped because I didn't want to take no for an answer. I just thought, "I can do it. It will be fine," such as moving my left side. I'm typing this right now, and I'm using both hands. I think that since I am determined and hardheaded I pushed through all the challenges and pain that I faced. Mom said I showed resilience, whatever that means.

How does it feel to know so many people, even those who have never met you, prayed for you?

It feels amazing. Everyone praying for me, getting me gifts, and visiting me meant so much. I really saw that when people come together and are just kind it can make others feel so loved. Even last week at church I was in the bathroom and a mom said to me at the sink, "My little girl has been praying for you." I didn't know their names, but they prayed for me. So many people took their own time to think of me and send up prayers, which just made me feel so loved.

When you reflect upon your accident and recovery, what stands out the most to you? Meaning, what lessons will you carry with you for the rest of your life as a result of your experience?

The lesson that I learned from the accident was that you should cherish each day because it can be taken from you in an instant. Also, love everyone, even if they make you mad (aka Henry).

Share your feelings about Winston's survival.

I always wanted a puppy, and the day that I got him was one of the best days of my life. To imagine that he wouldn't be here today would be horrible. I feel so joyful that he is still alive. Every day, I cuddle him and I like to take him on walks.

How has what happened to you impacted your life as a normal kid?

The accident impacted my life in many ways. Some of the sacrifices that I have had to make are dealing with a shaved head, not being allowed to play basketball and soccer because they are contact sports, and I can't ride any roller coasters for a whole entire year. I don't even understand why I can't play soccer and basketball. Soccer may be the sport with the highest risk of getting a concussion in girls' sports, but I've never gotten one, and why would I get one this year? I think I should be able to play basketball. Once I am cleared and allowed to play basketball and soccer and go on wild rides again, I think I will be more appreciative that I have these privileges. I won't take them for granted.

What was the most meaningful gift you received after your accident?

The word "gift" can mean many things. It may be a physical item or present. It can also be an ability or talent, but I think the greatest gift through all of this was the people who were involved and helped me; the people who prayed for me; the doctors, my friends, classmates, teachers, and priests; but especially my family. Without them I wouldn't have survived. So I'm not going to think of the "gift" in this question as a present wrapped up, but as people; because all the people who helped me were more important than the gifts. Without the doctors who operated on me I wouldn't have been fixed and wouldn't be able to do the processes needed for life. I owe everyone who was a part of helping me after the accident a huge thank you, because everyone was part of why I survived. From my family and doctors, even to the ambulance driver that got me to the hospital, they all played a part—big and small, so THANK YOU.

A Year Later

I woke up in the four o'clock hour thinking about snow skiing, wondering if that is still a viable vacation option for our family. My mind took off, racing through yesterday's conversation at Evelyn's one-year Rehabilitation Medicine follow-up appointment. We have all been waiting, eagerly anticipating with the fullest hearts, this one-year mark after her accident. It is the finish-line tape she is ready to triumphantly burst through at the end of this treacherous, year-long race. It has been a long wait. The liturgical season of Lent with its expectant and hopeful waiting has even greater significance to our family this year. Holy Saturday, tomorrow, marks one year since Evelyn's accident. God's timing is spectacular. What better way exists to rejoice at the gift of the risen Christ on Easter Sunday than by beginning a new year, afresh with a return to normal physical activities free of restrictions for Evelyn? However, being an optimist means that I sometimes get derailed when things do not go as I expect.

When life gives you lemons, make lemonade.

See the glass half-full.

Have an attitude of gratitude.

Wide awake in the still darkness of my bedroom before dawn, curled up for comfort behind my warm husband, I rolled these phrases concepts in which I find truth—through my mind. I want to feel fully thankful, but I'm so sad and disheartened. In God's plan, Christ died on the cross as the ultimate gift to humanity, providing the promise of eternal life for his followers. I ask myself what meaning I am supposed to find in our circumstances. What rough edges of my heart are supposed to be chiseled smooth through this part of our journey, and why must my child be the one forced to endure it? Yesterday, I wept. Today, I feel more like screaming or pounding my fists. I am strong. I can handle anything. I can parent my children deliberately, with loving guidance. However, I must first know the rules of the game to prepare them for how to exist within the limits we face.

At Evelyn's appointment, she passed her neurological and reflexes exams with flying colors. The warm physician went so far as to say, "I'm trying to find something, and I can't. There is no sign that anything happened to you. You're normal." She explained that Traumatic Brain Injury patients may possess good balance and strength, yet often upon careful examination there is some slight defect with a reflex. Some patients a year after TBI still have trouble with balance or walking. Not Evelyn. She is cured. She is coordinated. She is a picture of health.

But . . .

Sometimes there is a dreaded "but." This one drains my resolve to stay positive and strong. I know I will process it in time, yet in this early phase of contemplating the news, I hate it.

When the physician asked Evelyn if she had any questions about returning to activities, Ev did not say much. I jumped in and said to her, "Oh, yes you do! We've been waiting since April 20 for this day!" Sitting out of contact sports—namely soccer and basketball—was a cross to bear for Evelyn. She adores being with her friends, and playing team sports with them brings her great joy.

We received unexpected bad news. The doctor explained that depending upon whom you ask, rehabilitation medicine, sports medicine, and neurology experts will give different answers about patients returning to contact sports after TBI. It is gray area. The general consensus is that unlike putting a cast on a broken bone for a specified period of time, with a part of the body as vital as the brain, after TBI most physicians will recommend no return to contact sports—EVER.

Whoa. That statement took me by complete surprise and stopped my giddy anticipation of good news like cold water thrown in my face. My mind registered disbelief. I must have misheard. I simply looked at the physician in true shock. Then, I looked at my daughter. She is so strong—sometimes fierce. She was expressionless. Silent. She just sat there—stone cold and still. I knew the wheels were turning, and I anticipated a raging slew of defiant, angry, challenging words the moment we left the exam room. I started asking questions in an attempt to wrap my head around this news.

I was honest. I told the physician that last May we were told Evelyn was advised to sit out of contact sports for a year. We supported the physicians' recommendations, despite Evelyn's deep disappointment, in an effort to protect Evelyn's bruised, healing brain from secondary concussion and detrimental recovery setbacks. Never would I have led my child to believe that her restrictions would be lifted in a year if anyone had told me that was not the case. I felt naïve. Honestly, I felt like an idiot and a horrible mother. I turned to Evelyn, broke down, and told her how sorry I was, that I felt like I had failed her by aiming for the one-year mark as our ultimate target, never understanding the reality of life following a serious TBI. Evelyn said nothing. She stoically held back tears at the sight of my parental emotional outburst. I told the doctor that we are grateful for the blessing of Evelyn's remarkable recovery, but this news is our daughter's reality and impacts her everyday life and happiness.

We had a conversation similar to the one we had with a physician last May, but the bottom line remained the same. Another brain injury or concussion could result in a setback from which Evelyn may not recover. We agreed to table the matter until the next head CT scan on April 30. We will see how Dr. Kaufman weighs in on the conversation.

Surprisingly, Evelyn said nothing as we left the office and made our way out of the hospital. She kept her composure until our drive home when we called Robbie on Bluetooth. I gave him a report of Evelyn's checkup. I respect my husband's wisdom. As I broke down and sobbed, he said, "Julie, middle-school and high-school contact sports are short-lived compared to using her brain for a lifetime." I knew he was right. Evelyn hung her head with her forehead resting in her palm and wept as I drove with tears streaming down my face. Once again, flung back to last spring, I could do nothing to alleviate my child's hurt, frustration, and dejection.

All around us there is real suffering within arm's reach. A neighbor friend's in-utero baby boy has a heart defect that will necessitate surgeries and a potentially challenging prognosis. A neighbor's friend's young son was recently diagnosed with a brain tumor and endured neurosurgery. A close friend's cousin, mother to two young children, is on a ventilator with lung complications from chemotherapy used to treat invasive colorectal cancer. A friend's father-in-law is in critical condition with heart problems. The sweet little girl two doors down has leukemia and has been battling it for over a year with a two-year maintenance phase still to go. Each example represents genuine human struggle and provides opportunities for prayer, faith, hope, and trust.

The complexity of local, American, and global problems facing society's most vulnerable through the modern-day slavery of human sex trafficking is a real and widespread example of horrific suffering. Encouraged by friends to view *Nefarious—Merchant of Souls*, a documentary produced by Exodus Cry, I finally had the courage to remove my head from the sand to learn about the appalling problems endured by millions of worldwide children, girls, and women trapped in the modern-day, sickening, forced prostitution of those exploited and sold for sex. The magnitude of that problem and the layers of corruption and violence protecting it seem insurmountable. The depths of suffering the victims experience in the face of such true evil is gut-wrenching. Yet, still we maintain hope for an end to this injustice. We hope on! We may individually get involved to intervene through community action and the power of prayer. "A person changed by prayer can change the world," for nothing is impossible for God (from *Meeting Christ in Prayer*).

My dad says, "There is plenty of suffering to go around." I know every person reading this book has encountered suffering and sees it in our world. I can rationally recognize how, in light of more serious health and world matters, to outside observers we have a perfectly restored child with a healthy life and boundless opportunities ahead of her. I know Evelyn wants to play certain sports, yet she has access to myriad other options. I agree that when the world closes one door, God opens others. I realize my mindset may appear selfish or shallow. I am honestly sharing our woes because large or small, they affect us and hurt. They impact my child. Again, I must ask myself if I honestly trust in the Lord—not just when I'm blessed and things are easy, but when his plan is not the plan I would choose. That's true faith.

We will keep walking, one foot in front of the other. We will keep processing all the experiences that have come from Evelyn's accident. Tomorrow, we will celebrate survival and strength and faith and beauty and grit. We will praise God for Evelyn's life. We will love one another and cherish each moment. We will look on the bright side and count our many blessings because we believe God is good—ever confident that God's will is never more than his grace will allow.

Accident Anniversary
· · · · · · · · · · · · · · · · · · · *Holy Saturday, April 20, 2019*

Today is a little sliver of perfection in our flawed world. The weather is as splendid as a sublime California day. Spring blossoms delight us on trees, the colorful tulips in our landscaping sway in the breeze, and I watch Evelyn bask in the warm sunshine on our back patio, enjoying time with her siblings, with her puppy nearby. We are enjoying a leisurely morning, and Evelyn is happy to consume sweet pastries for breakfast.

Shortly after noon, our doorbell rings. Heather Coones, a Curé mom and talented Botanica floral designer, delivers a spectacular vase of flowers to Evelyn from her friends. Heather warns me that the card will make me cry, and she is correct. "Evelyn—we are so grateful for your friendship and are proud of your perseverance during your recovery this year. We are amazed that something so awful could make you even more beautiful. A year ago we begged God to heal you, and today we thank God for you! We have so much to celebrate. With love, Anna, Maggie, Macy, Lily, Catherine, Ava and Lauryn."

I enjoy fresh flowers so much that we grow cut flowers, zinnias and sunflowers, in our backyard garden each summer, and with entrepreneurial spirit our kids run a *Backyard Blooms* summer business selling floral bouquets to neighbors—their own take on a lemonade stand. The flowers Evelyn receives are my favorite shades of spring: exquisite, pale-yellow ranunculus; sunshine-yellow Star of Bethlehem; pale-coral Gerbera daisies; blush-pink roses, and little lavender blooms with delicate, white crab-apple blossoms. We feel delighted by the sight of the gorgeous flowers, and the gift is a beautiful display of loving friendship and support from the girls and their mothers. I tell Heather, "These women never cease to amaze me." Incredible.

⌇

Evelyn's first-grade teacher, Mrs. Lorraine Silkman, spent class time praying the Rosary with her students. That sparked a beautiful prayer life in my little girl that year. It was not uncommon for Evelyn to pray the Rosary on her own in our home before bedtime. On a visit to our Catholic bookstore, Trinity House, the next year, Evelyn spotted a very large statue (28 inches tall and 13 inches in diameter) of the Blessed Mother holding infant Jesus. With $25 of First Communion gift money in her pocket, Evelyn said, "I want to buy her," as she pointed to Mary and baby Jesus. I explained to my child that the gorgeous statue was nearly ten times the amount of money she had available. "We can't always get what we want."

Evelyn is nothing if not determined, even as a little girl in elementary school. She started saving birthday and Christmas gift money from generous grandparents and asked to perform extra household chores to earn cash. Purchasing the stunning statue was her ultimate goal. Late the following year, her funds had grown; but not surprisingly, given the expense of the statue, she was not quite there. Two of her siblings kindly offered to contribute their own money to make Evelyn's dream come true.

I suspect you can imagine how it made my heart sing to return to the bookstore to buy the tall statue. Thankfully, it was still there! God wink. As Evelyn stepped to the counter and passed her stack of bills up to the cashier, I shared the backstory. The store owner, Bob Shea, was called to the front; touched by Evelyn's sweet heart, he granted a discount. We took home Mother Mary, dressed in a splendid, blue robe, with sweet baby Jesus held lovingly in maternal arms. Her gaze is one of fond tenderness to her infant son. His pose and expression show peace and security. Mary delights in baby Jesus. That was a high point in my life as a mother. This statue of the gentle mother resides in Evelyn and Vivian's shared bedroom, and I feel peace when I look at it. To me, Mary is the ultimate example of motherly love.

Fast-forward to the weeks leading up to the one-year mark of Evelyn's accident. I prayed the Rosary early each morning while playing the Holy Family School of Faith Daily Rosary Meditations podcast recorded by Dr. Mike Scherschligt as I prepared breakfast for my family. At the end of each Rosary, he encourages listeners, "Be apostles of the Rosary. Share this with others." For a few mornings in a row, Mike welcomed listeners to email him an invitation to lead a Rosary for them as they gathered friends for conversation and prayer. I thought about it, then even though we had never met, I decided to reach out to him about leading a Rosary on the anniversary of Evelyn's accident, which would amazingly fall on Holy Saturday, April 20, 2019.

In yet another God wink, although I did not receive a response to my initial email invitation and lengthy description of the details surrounding April 20, through Divine intervention and the fortuitous assistance of Adrienne, not many days prior to Saturday, I discovered I was in fact on Mike Scherschligt's calendar for a Rosary recording April 20. Plans were solidified to meet in the church, and I extended an invitation to our community to join us in person or in the spirit of prayer. Understandably, many friends had plans to travel for Easter, were hosting guests for the holiday weekend, and had kids' sporting events to juggle that Saturday afternoon. Countless friends offered to pray from afar in gratitude for Evelyn's wonderful healing and amazing recovery.

The church was decorated for Easter when we arrived. Our life-sized crucifix had a long, white drape of cloth behind it, and floral arrangements with tulips and hydrangeas decorated the altar in colors of springtime. It was stunning.

Our family was blessed with the presence of Grandpa Tom and Grandma Jane from Springfield, Illinois; Uncle Anthony and Aunt Megan Niedzielski from Dallas, Texas; and Megan's local parents and aunt, Ron and Alice Ross and Carol Halter. Our dearest friends and neighbors, including the Hills, Katie and Maggie, and Ashley and Lauryn; Catholic Scripture Study ladies; and many other supportive individuals joined us. There were several teachers present along with classmates of my children with their parents. Similar to the joy we experienced the day of Vivian's First Communion/Evelyn's Survival Mass, we were overwhelmed by the outpouring of loving and prayerful support. There were even people present we had never met. They simply heard about the Rosary and attended to pray with us.

At Mike's request, but with just a few minutes to collect my thoughts and calm my nerves, I shared with those gathered that I prayed the Hail Mary on April 20, 2018, as I held Evelyn in the grass immediately following the accident, when her outcome was uncertain. Her friends and their mothers prayed the Rosary during her urgent surgery. Full circle, one year later, we prayed the Rosary again and recognized the intervention of the Mother of God in the healing through her Son of one of God's precious children, our Evelyn. Mike led the Rosary with uplifting, truly inspiring meditations after each decade. Since it is recorded the previous day for the next day's podcast, on Holy Saturday we prayed aloud the Easter Sunday Rosary. Everyone expressed the sentiment that our prayers were a beautiful way to show honor to God in thanksgiving for all his many blessings in our lives. We were grateful for God's goodness and grace. I am grateful to have a recording preserved of my family and friends praying together.

Later that special day, our four children dyed Easter eggs—with minimal bickering, cracking, and staining. We took our family and relatives out to Evelyn's favorite Mexican restaurant, Cactus Grill, for a celebratory dinner. We attended the sacred 7:00 PM Mass of the Easter Vigil in the Holy Night—Resurrection of the Lord. It began in solemn darkness, then from the paschal candle, the stunning Lucernarium (Service of Light) began, and one by one, each person's candle was lit—the physical and symbolic lighting of the new fire. The Mass was moving as we sang "Alleluia." During the Prayer of the Faithful, Sr. Julie Galan, a fixture at Curé, read that the Mass was said for the intentions of Evelyn Overlease, which caused my daughter to give me a meek smile with a twinkle in her eyes. Attending the Easter Vigil was the perfect way to bring Lent and Evelyn's year of recovery to a close. We rejoiced at the blessing of the risen Christ and the hope that fills our hearts as followers.

Easter Sunday morning, ten of us celebrated a beautiful Mass together, feasted on homemade brunch, hunted Easter eggs, consumed too much candy, spent hours in good conversation, and ate our ham dinner on my Grandma Fabiana Niedzielski's china. It was a perfect Easter day.

But . . .

Our story got better.

God's ways are mysterious, and we received another gift on Easter Monday. Before bedtime I checked email. I discovered a note from CMH from a Rehabilitation Medicine doctor. She retracted her recommendation that Evelyn not return to contact sports. Upon reviewing Evelyn's case with colleagues and further reviewing relevant literature, for which I was grateful, the determination was made that in light of how well Evelyn has done with her recovery, it would be okay for her to return to soccer and basketball. The risk is less as we move beyond the date of the accident. "So, I would like to change my prior statement about Evelyn playing sports. After one year, the risks are lower in someone who has recovered so well. It is ultimately your decision knowing the potential risks we discussed in clinic, but from my perspective, as long as her CT scan looks good and Dr. Kaufman is ok with it, she can return to play after the one-year mark."

Imagine my awe! I grabbed my laptop and raced to Robbie. He silently read the note, and we agreed to keep this positive news private until a definitive answer is reached April 30. However, again, God cannot be outdone in his mercy and generosity. We must trust God's holy will and his perfect timing. Did the power of prayer from our Rosary cause a ripple that led to the physical-activities clearance for which Evelyn so longed? I do not know the answer. His ways are beyond our comprehension. And so, coinciding with the hopeful joys Christians of the world encounter at

Easter, my daughter shall now embark on a spectacular season of her new life after facing an unexpected challenge, enduring the hardship of pain, and patiently awaiting full healing and medical release. Evelyn is now a thriving thirteen-year-old, a teenager. Blessings abound. We sing the praises of the glory of God in all his miraculous works.

. . . . *April 30, 2019*

We received fantastic news at Evelyn's one-year neurosurgery follow-up appointment. A CT revealed complete bone healing where she had endured multiple fractures, including a significant depressed skull fracture, surgical decompression, and fixation of her broken skull. The goal was for everything to fuse to form one solid skull, which indeed happened. Alleluia! However, it was quite surprising, even shocking, to see the 3D images of her head in its current state. As serious as I knew her depressed skull fracture injury was, Evelyn's healed skull looks worse on the CT images, more complicated and irregular from corrective surgery to repair the damage, than my mind's eye envisioned. After recovering from TBI, the CT shows Evelyn has a healthy brain!

When Evelyn and I touch her scalp, we are able to feel lines of bony ridges and some lumpy projections. Upon reviewing the CT, those areas are bumpy ridges where the bone is calcifying through the ossifying process of healing. Dr. Kaufman said those areas will become smoother in two to three years; the human body is amazing. Evelyn has two dog-bone-shaped and two square, permanent, titanium microplates used to secure the elevated bone flap; we are able to feel two of these metal pieces. After twelve months, Evelyn has been blessed with complete bone fusion. I maintain that I always knew she was hardheaded.

Evelyn is cleared to return to physical activity without restriction! Based on her healing, Dr. Kaufman said it is fine for Evelyn to play female contact sports (such as soccer and basketball) and to participate in snow skiing and sledding. She must wear a helmet while participating in sports/activities that require a helmet, such as biking. He said holding patients out of activities has a longer lifetime detriment than the risk of allowing them to play. The data show that after fully healing, a patient's participation in contact sports poses no increased risk. Evelyn is fortunate that no portion of her brain had to be removed. If that was the case, among other serious implications, there would be empty space in her skull that could allow the brain to slam around upon impact from a fall or collision. Evelyn may proceed through life and resume activities with the understanding that there are certain risks inherent to specific sports and activities. She received a great medical report and is released from the care of Dr. Kaufman.

Naturally, I was thrilled with Dr. Kaufman's report. Evelyn did not show much of a reaction to the "all clear" assessment and medical release for participation in all physical activities. Perhaps she needs time to process this new plan for freedom. She seems guarded, as though she is not quite ready to allow herself to fully experience excitement about the prospect of living life as she did before her accident. She has had to grapple with a range of emotions over the last year, and I must remind myself that she is still young.

Right after Evelyn's accident, if someone had asked me to write the story of the year ahead, I could not have come up with a more positive outcome. I suspect Evelyn's perfect version of her story would include hair that regrew to full length, but we are grateful for the six to seven inches of hair growth in the large shaved area. Everyone loves a happy ending. Thankfully, through the grace of God, we are living one! Our family has experienced many God winks on our amazing journey. We grew in faith, hope, and love, and Evelyn experienced a complete recovery and full bodily healing without residual defects. What better outcomes exist for mere humans? We will continue to count our multitude of blessings and give Almighty God the credit for walking hand in hand with us every step of the way. We never fight the hard battles alone.

I leave you with encouragement to go forward with trust that God is love, and ultimately, he will bring good from ALL things. From the depths of my soul I believe the spiritual importance of the following:

Have faith. Hope on! God is good.

Photos of Evelyn's Story

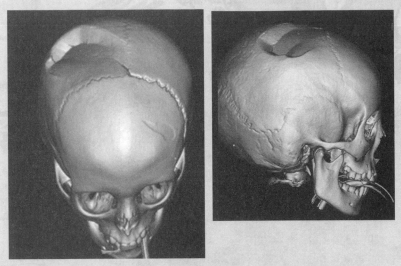

Evelyn Overlease's Head CT Scan 4/20/18, compressed skull fracture
and coronal suture fracture—intubated.

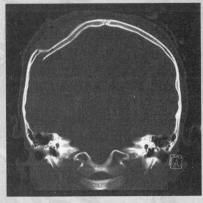

Bone shard in the area of
Evelyn's motor cortex

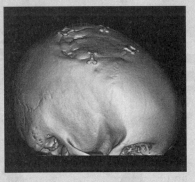

April 2019, 1-year post-op
CT of repaired skull

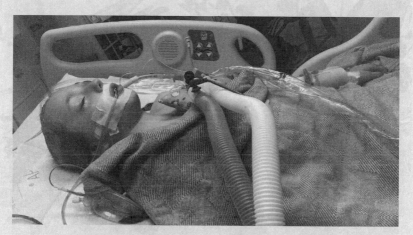

This was our first look at Evelyn late in the evening 4/20/18.

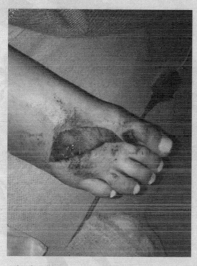

The limb severed the leather strap on Evelyn's sandal.

This was our daughter's awful reality post-operation, and yet this outcome was a blessing.

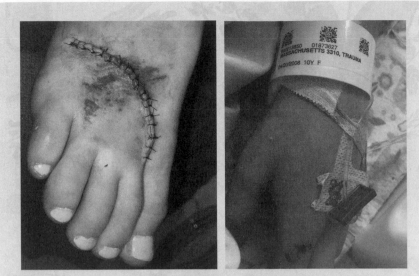

35 stitches in multiple layers

Evelyn Overlease,
aka Trauma Massachusetts

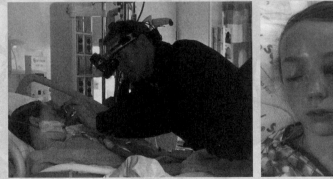

Evelyn's dad, an ophthalmologist, examined her
retina after the resident checked her in the PICU.
4/21/18

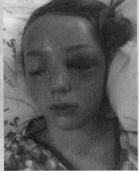

Swollen from IV fluids

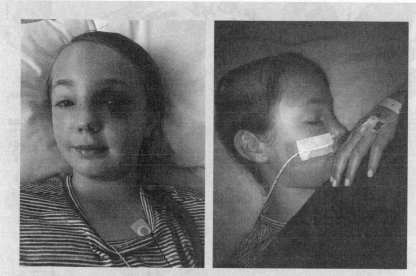

Black eye from orbital roof fracture—
We were thrilled once Evelyn could
open her eye and wear her own
clothes. 4/24/18

4/25/18

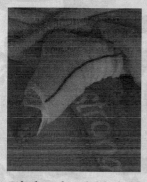

Gifts from friends lifted our
spirits in the hospital.

4/25/18

Evelyn was reunited with Winston during
Josie Finlason's CMH visit. 4/26/18

Emily Finlason brought Winston
to visit Evelyn.

Our delightful homecoming, 4/27/18

Julie's notebook

Saturday, 4/28/18 - Vivian's First Communion/Evelyn's
Survival Mass with grandparents (L to R: Mary and
Mike Conlon, Tom and Jane Niedzielski)
PHOTO CREDIT: Adrienne Doring

Kids left to right: Olivia, Evelyn,
Vivian, Henry
PHOTO CREDIT: Adrienne Doring

Fr. Richard Storey, Curé of Ars Pastor
PHOTO CREDIT: Adrienne Doring

Winston at Church
PHOTO CREDIT: Adrienne Doring

PHOTO CREDIT: Adrienne Doring

Julie with Jane Hill
PHOTO CREDIT: Adrienne Doring

PHOTO CREDIT: Adrienne Doring

This gives an impression of what I saw
when I rushed to the privacy fence.
PHOTO CREDIT: Adrienne Doring

"Hey Mom! Where's my tennis shoe?"

Evelyn revisited the yard 5/4/18
(2 weeks after the accident) as a survivor.
PHOTO CREDIT: Adrienne Doring

Cell phone image taken at scene of
the accident

PHOTO CREDIT: Adrienne Doring

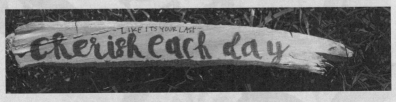

Track baton award from Notre Dame de Sion High School
PHOTO CREDIT: Adrienne Doring

Penned by Evelyn on wood from the tree
PHOTO CREDIT: Adrienne Doring

A gift to Evelyn from Maggie Axtell
PHOTO CREDIT: Adrienne Doring

Maggie Axtell and Evelyn
with turkey feet, April 2014

Frisco, Colorado vacation—
July 2018

Junior Tennis League doubles partners
7/16/18, Anna Gillespie and Evelyn

Overlease family, October 2018—Vivian, Evelyn, Julie, Robbie, Olivia, Henry & Winston
PHOTO CREDIT: Angie Lee Photography

Evelyn's puppy brings her joy. God is good.
PHOTO CREDIT: Angie Lee Photography

7th grade track, Spring 2019

Mount Royal summit, July 30, 2018

Evelyn purchased this statue as a little girl.

Curé Soirée 2019—Chris and Jane Hill,
Overleases, Jenny and Mike McGinnis,
Sarah and Marc Parrish
(not pictured: Katie and Paul Axtell)

Accident anniversary,
Holy Saturday, 4/20/19
—With family, left to right: Anthony,
Tom, Megan, and Jane Niedzielski

October 2018

Unexpected, Extended Hospital-Stay Survival Items

Our kind friends swooped in and met needs that we did not realize we had, and their generous giving made being in the hospital a more pleasant and tolerable experience. I wish to share the following list should you ever have the opportunity to bless someone in their time of crisis.

- Notebook/journal and a good pen for medical notetaking
- Holy water
- Soft toilet paper
- Basic toiletries: toothbrush, toothpaste, body wash, deodorant, nail clippers/file
- Luxurious hand cream, lip balm, gum, mints
- Rapid phone charger with extra-long cable
- Inspirational small signs or cards
- Painter's tape (to hang signs and cards)
- Fluffy pillow and cozy blanket for the caregiver
- Creature comforts that are a daily routine (for me: morning coffee)
- Reading material
- Snacks: roasted nuts, protein bars, apples, washed fresh berries, hard-boiled eggs, candy treats, herbal teabags, or healthy bottled drinks

Acknowledgments

This book would not be possible without God's blessing of Evelyn's life. He is good. I humbly thank him for sparing my little girl's life. Evelyn's openness to the idea of allowing me to share the details of her story and graphic photos of her injuries was paramount to allowing the call that I heard to write this book to move forward. Thank you for being a confident, gracious, loving, and trusting daughter, Evelyn. I have so much love, admiration, and respect for you. May you continue to use the gifts you have received and live out God's wonderful purpose for your life. You are an amazing girl, and I am so pleased to be your mother. You hold the attitude that everything is up for negotiation, but that fire in your spirit makes you strong. It is a key part of your essence. That tree didn't stand a chance. You are a true force to be reckoned with, and I will continue to pray for your future spouse. Dad and I love you so much. Your siblings are thankful for your survival.

Thank you to each of our parents and stepparents for your unconditional love and support over the course of a lifetime. Love begets love. You have blessed us richly.

I would like to thank all the people who encouraged me to take my medical-update emails and turn them into a story to share news of God's goodness and glory. Without your words, "You should write a book," April 20 would become a fading memory. Now, the God winks of the full story may live on, and Evelyn has the gift of the full story from various angles to process, reflect upon, and share with the people yet to enter her life. God's mercy and love overflowed, and I am thrilled to honor him by sharing our experience. This project was an emotionally taxing endeavor, and I wish to thank my loving family for their support during the long writing process. Olivia, you never cease to amaze me at the outstanding woman you have become. Thank you for suggesting "Impact" as part of the title. I am confident every soul who reads our story perceives the multifaceted, amazing ways the accident touched many individuals.

Thank you to the fine women of the Curé of Ars Catholic Scripture Study for so freely sharing your hearts and nuggets of life's wisdom within our group. Together, we form a unique sisterhood of faith that is an uncommon blessing. Your prayers meant the world to us, and being in fellowship with you as we study Scripture adds great richness to my faith. Your friendship enhances my life. I love you.

I wish to thank Jon Sweeney of Paraclete Press for his quick response to my unsolicited manuscript submission. I am not a writer, but a mom with a story to share. He blessed me by taking a chance on a never-before-published author, and I am immeasurably grateful. Each professional from Paraclete Press with whom I have had the pleasure of working has been warm and caring. They are more than competent staff members at a publisher—they are exemplary people. Their guidance made the publication process enjoyable.

Upon beginning a volunteer endeavor at a crisis pregnancy center, I discovered that another Client Advocate is the mother of a young paramedic on Evelyn's ambulance call. I was instantly horrified thinking about my harrowing written account of our ambulance ride. Her son was working on Evelyn in the ambulance with another man. When I shared this surprising news with my family, Vivian asked, "Do you think he told his mom you were crazy?" "YES!" was my emphatic, wholehearted reply. So, to the men on board the ambulance, thank you for your efforts to help Evelyn. I am grateful to first responders. I humbly ask you to please empathize with my frantic parental fear and forgive my agitation.

Thank you, Ashley and Tim Murphy, for contacting Fr. Storey to expediently get him to the hospital to meet us, and for facilitating our keeping our previously scheduled April 27 dinner plans with him. Father, your blessing, prayers, and support in arranging an impromptu First Communion/Evelyn's Survival Mass will never be forgotten. It was splendid.

Even in her fragile state, sweet Evelyn recognized the gift of the day Emily Finlason lovingly spent serving us in the hospital room. "Mom, she's so nice," Evelyn gratefully commented. Emily was the wheels of the mission to retrieve Winston from the veterinary hospital to brighten Evelyn's day with a visit from her beloved puppy at the hospital. Our mental mindsets are powerful instruments of bodily healing. Emily's efforts to bring Evelyn joy were instrumental in helping her turn a corner in the hospital. She was discharged the day after Winston's delightful visit.

Katie Axtell and Allie Goodman, it was so helpful and kind of you to contact Athleta, Birkenstock, and Vineyard Vines on Evelyn's behalf. Each company kindly replaced the twelfth-birthday gift items Evelyn was wearing that were destroyed by the accident and in the ambulance and hospital during life-saving emergency measures. She had those special items for a mere two weeks prior to April 20. Susan Fronczak's warmth and kind gestures to Evelyn in the Country Club Plaza Vineyard Vines store while processing an exchange will always be fondly remembered. We connected, mother to mother.

Everyone associated with Children's Mercy Hospital deserves the ultimate compliment for the professionalism and skill with which they care for pediatric patients. First, we are immeasurably grateful to Dr. Ashley Daly-Murphy for calling in the trauma team from the Goodmans' yard. "Thank you" is inadequate to express our deep gratitude to all the surgeons, physicians, social workers, nurses, and therapists whose work led to saving Evelyn's life and then to a positive recovery. Dr. Kaufman, thank you for leaving the little strip of hair that framed Evelyn's forehead and temple when you had to shave her head. That act of forethought made a difference in her self-confidence during a rocky time emotionally. God bless you! As an expression of gratitude for Evelyn's outstanding medical care, a portion of proceeds will be donated to benefit Children's Mercy Facility Dog Program. Evelyn's puppy's hospital visit lifted her spirits, and we want to give other young patients the gift of time spent enjoying therapy dogs.

Allie Goodman and Kelli Martin, thank you for your concern for the welfare of our puppy and your quick-thinking actions to seek emergency treatment for him. Mission Road Animal Clinic and Mission Veterinary Emergency both provided fine care, and the flowers each office sent were beautiful gestures of support and kindness.

Robbie, Olivia, Jane Hill, Emily Claxton, Carol Halter, Ron Ross, Dad, and Jane—I appreciate your willingness to read and critique my manuscript. Angie Henderson, thank you for your professional read and detailed, constructive editing. I trusted you to be frank with me, and true to your nature, you did not disappoint.

Many heartfelt thanks extend to every person responsible for blessing us with messages, cards, beautiful flowers, thoughtful gifts, food (homemade bread, protein shakes, desserts), delicious meals, and prayers. Thank you to Jenny McGinnis for organizing the sign-up for nutritious meals for our family, allowing me to focus on Evelyn, instead of on cooking. It was humbling to contemplate the breadth of care and kind actions so many people lovingly bestowed upon our family. The Lourdes holy water from the Kernells, Sextons, and Leonards was used repeatedly to bless Evelyn in the hospital. Henry attributes his sister's healing to the blessing he provided with your holy gift. Thank you. Dr. Natasha Burgert, your sincere and heartfelt voice message upon learning of Evelyn's accident truly showed the deep level of your love and concern for Evelyn and our family. You made a house call to save us a trip to your office. You are an amazing and one-of-a-kind doctor.

Thank you to Mr. Greer, Mrs. Palmer, Mrs. Wank, and Evelyn's sixth-grade classmates for the crazy, upbeat, YouTube get-well video and cards. Laughter was rare in the first two weeks after the accident, yet you brightened Evelyn's mood immensely.

Adrienne Doring, your photography at First Communion and in the Goodmans' backyard was such an unexpected, yet delightful, blessing. Thank you for capturing such meaningful moments for our family. You forever preserved our wondrous joy in the wake of enduring a hardship. As a mother of four young children with limited free time, it was especially kind of you to photograph other items, such as the baton and wood from the tree, for inclusion in this book.

Mary Leonard, bless you for your forethought to bring the Eucharist to CMH the Sunday we were in the PICU. The Bread of Life strengthened us. Katie and Maggie Axtell, the gift of your vivid, beautiful letter to Evelyn was priceless. Maggie, we value your bravery sharing your harrowing account of the accident when you visited the hospital and in your written words.

Not to be forgotten, for hot, much-needed coffee delivered to Evelyn's hospital room—thank you Becky Pepin, Ashley Murphy, and Jamie Hess. Girls from the accident: Evelyn's "Jesus, I Trust in You" embroidered, blue fleece blanket and guest room makeover made her feel incredibly loved and comfortable. Thank you to the mothers of the girls for organizing the Card My Yard sign to welcome us home. This accident formed a bond among the young friends and their fine mothers that will always remain. Let it serve as a reminder of the importance of prayer, trusting God with hope, and compassionately serving one another with love.

I am grateful to the 2018/2019 soccer and basketball coaches, Brian Gillespie, Brian McDaniel, Michael Mason, and Tim Murphy, for inviting Evelyn to join the team during practices in a noncontact capacity. Their generous inclusion was a social blessing.

Angie Lee Photography blessed us in October 2018, once Evelyn's hair had regrown enough that my daughter was comfortable with the idea of a family photo for our Christmas card. Angie put us at ease, made us laugh, and captured the joy of our intact family.

Thank you, Mike Scherschligt of the School of Faith, for leading the Rosary at Curé of Ars Church on the anniversary of Evelyn's accident. It is a tremendous gift to possess an audio recording of family members and friends praying aloud in thanksgiving for Evelyn's blessings, and we will always treasure it.

Finally, Robbie . . . I nearly lost you a few months before Evelyn's accident after your blood clot. I think God knew how much I needed you to hold my hand on our unplanned walk with Evelyn. You mean everything to me. I promise to love you and honor you all the days of my life. I'm so happy you are mine.

American Authors. "Best Day of My Life." Accetta, Aaron. Barnett, Zachary. Goodman, Shep. Rublin, David. Sanchez, Matthew. Shelley, James. *Oh, What a Life*. Universal Island Records, 2012, 3.

Children's Mercy Hospital, Brain Injury Manual.

Excerpts from *Daring to Hope: Finding God's Goodness in the Broken and the Beautiful* by Katie Davis Majors, copyright © 2017 by Katie Davis Majors. Used by permission of WaterBrook Multnomah, an imprint of Random House, a division of Penguin Random House LLC. All rights reserved.

Glynn, Paul. *Song for Nagasaki—The Story of Takashi Nagai: Scientist, Convert, and Survivor of the Atomic Bomb*. San Francisco: Ignatius Press, 2009.

Guetta, David. "Titanium." *Nothing but the Beat*. Virgin, 2011, 13.

Lyrics reprinted by permission: "You are Mine" by David Haas. Used by permission of GIA Publications, Inc. [copyright © 1991].

McBratney, Sam. *You're All My Favorites*. Cambridge, MA: Candlewick Press, 2007.

Nouwen, Henry J. M. *Life of the Beloved—Spiritual Living in a Secular World*. New York: Crossroads, 2018.

Norbet, Gregory. "Hosea." Benedictine Foundation of the State of Vermont, Inc. Printed with complimentary permission from the Brothers of Weston Priory.

"For Courage" from *To Bless the Space Between Us: A Book of Blessings* by John O'Donohue, copyright © 2008 by John O'Donohue. Used by permission of Doubleday, an imprint of the Knopf Doubleday Publishing Group, a division of Penguin Random House LLC. All rights reserved.

Philippe, Fr. Jacques. *Searching for and Maintaining Peace—A Small Treatise on Peace of Heart*. New York: Society of St. Paul, 2002.

Platten, Rachel. "Stand by You." Platten, Rachel. Antonoff, Jack. Williams, Joy. Morris, Matt. Levine, Jon. *Wildfire*. Columbia Records, 2015, 2.

Rowling, J. K. *Harry Potter and the Prisoner of Azkaban*. New York: Scholastic, 1999.

Sassani, John E., McLaughlin, Mary Anne. *Meeting Christ in Prayer—An 8-Week Life-Enriching Experience Based on the Spiritual Exercises of St. Ignatius*. Chicago: Loyola Press, 2008.

About Paraclete Press

Who We Are

As the publishing arm of the Community of Jesus, Paraclete Press presents a full expression of Christian belief and practice—from Catholic to Evangelical, from Protestant to Orthodox, reflecting the ecumenical charism of the Community and its dedication to sacred music, the fine arts, and the written word. We publish books, recordings, sheet music, and video/DVDs that nourish the vibrant life of the church and its people.

What We Are Doing

BOOKS | PARACLETE PRESS BOOKS show the richness and depth of what it means to be Christian. While Benedictine spirituality is at the heart of who we are and all that we do, our books reflect the Christian experience across many cultures, time periods, and houses of worship.

We have many series, including *Paraclete Essentials*; *Paraclete Fiction*; *Paraclete Poetry*; *Paraclete Giants*; and for children and adults, *All God's Creatures*, books about animals and faith; and *San Damiano Books*, focusing on Franciscan spirituality. Others include *Voices from the Monastery* (men and women monastics writing about living a spiritual life today), *Active Prayer*, and new for young readers: *The Pope's Cat*. We also specialize in gift books for children on the occasions of Baptism and First Communion, as well as other important times in a child's life, and books that bring creativity and liveliness to any adult spiritual life.

The MOUNT TABOR BOOKS series focuses on the arts and literature as well as liturgical worship and spirituality; it was created in conjunction with the Mount Tabor Ecumenical Centre for Art and Spirituality in Barga, Italy.

MUSIC | The PARACLETE RECORDINGS label represents the internationally acclaimed choir *Gloriæ Dei Cantores*, the *Gloriæ Dei Cantores Schola*, and the other instrumental artists of the *Arts Empowering Life Foundation*.

Paraclete Press is the exclusive North American distributor for the Gregorian chant recordings from St. Peter's Abbey in Solesmes, France. Paraclete also carries all of the Solesmes chant publications for Mass and the Divine Office, as well as their academic research publications.

In addition, PARACLETE PRESS SHEET MUSIC publishes the work of today's finest composers of sacred choral music, annually reviewing over 1,000 works and releasing between 40 and 60 works for both choir and organ.

VIDEO | Our video/DVDs offer spiritual help, healing, and biblical guidance for a broad range of life issues including grief and loss, marriage, forgiveness, facing death, understanding suicide, bullying, addictions, Alzheimer's, and Christian formation.

Learn more about us at our website:
www.paracletepress.com
or phone us toll-free at 1.800.451.5006

SCAN
TO
READ
MORE

Other Personal Accounts of Loss and Hope

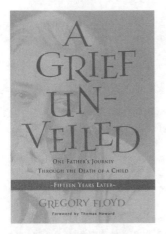

A Grief Unveiled
*One Father's Journey
Through the Death of a Child*
Gregory Floyd

ISBN 978-1-61261-239-3 | $18.99 | Trade paperback

A candid account of sudden grief and faith that has inspired thousands. Gregory Floyd's journey through grief after the tragic death of his youngest son recounts the full impact of such a loss on a typical Catholic family. He allows the reader into his heart as he grapples with emotions that question the goodness of God in the midst of unbearable grief.

"An extraordinary account…at once emotionally devastating, at times spirituality exhilarating, and most of the time both at once." —*First Things*

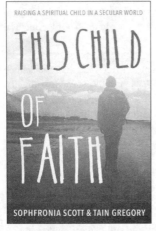

This Child of Faith
*Raising a Spiritual Child
in a Secular World*
Sophfronia Scott and Tain Gregory

ISBN 978-1-61261-925-5 | $16.99 | Trade paperback

Tain Gregory was present in this third-grade classroom on the morning of the Sandy Hook shootings. As part of the healing process after the tragedy, Tain was asked, "What's the most important thing in the world to you?" Tain thought for a moment, then answered with one word: "God."

"In this beautiful and timely memoir, mother and son share insights from a journey that led to a deeper experience of God. They tackle a difficult question: how does faith prepare us not only for life's joys but for its most shocking tragedies?" —DIANA BUTLER BASS

Available at bookstores
Paraclete Press | 1-800-451-5006
www.paracletepress.com